NO ORDINARY MOMENT

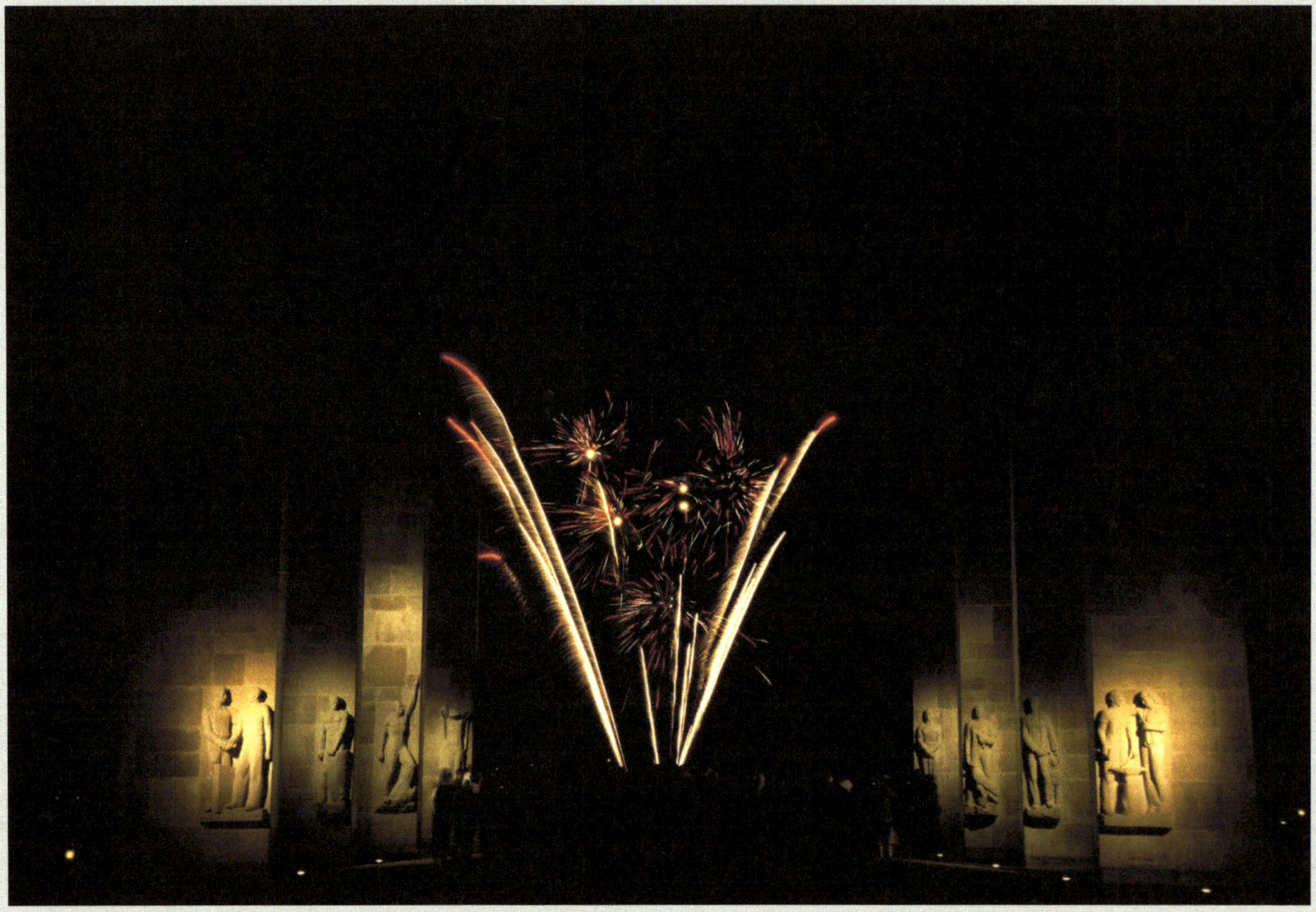

NO ORDINARY MOMENT

VIRGINIA TECH, 150 YEARS IN 150 IMAGES

AARON D. PURCELL, LM ROZEMA, ANTHONY WRIGHT DE HERNANDEZ, AND JOHN M. JACKSON

Virginia Tech Publishing | Blacksburg, Virginia | *Distributed by the University of Virginia Press*

Copyright © 2022 Aaron D. Purcell, LM Rozema, Anthony Wright de Hernandez, and John M. Jackson

First published 2022 by Virginia Tech Publishing

VIRGINIA TECH PUBLISHING
University Libraries at Virginia Tech
560 Drillfield Drive
Blacksburg, VA 24061

DISTRIBUTED BY THE UNIVERSITY OF VIRGINIA PRESS

(cc) BY-NC

This work is licensed under the Creative Commons Attribution-NonCommercial 4.0 International License. To view a copy of this license, visit http://creativecommons.org/licenses/by-nc/4.0/ or send a letter to Creative Commons, PO Box 1866, Mountain View, California, 94042, USA. Note to users: This work may contain components (e.g., photographs, illustrations, or quotations) not covered by the license. Every effort has been made to identify these components, but ultimately it is your responsibility to independently evaluate the copyright status of any work or component part of a work you use, in light of your intended use.

Cataloging-in-Publication Data
Names: Purcell, Aaron D. – author. | Rozema, LM – author. | Wright de Hernandez, Anthony – author. – | Jackson, John M. Jr. – author.
Title: No ordinary moment: Virginia Tech, 150 years in 150 images.
Description: Blacksburg, VA : Virginia Tech Publishing, 2022. | Distributed by the University of Virginia Press. | Includes bibliographical references. | Summary: A history of Virginia Tech, from its mid-nineteenth-century origins as Virginia Agricultural and Military College to present-day comprehensive research university with a global land-grant mission. The book features approximately 150 illustrations, including rare photographs and unique items from the Special Collections and University Archives at Virginia Tech and other campus sources. —Provided by publisher.
Identifiers: ISBN: 978-1-957213-16-3 (pbk) | ISBN: 978-1-957213-06-4 (PDF)| ISBN: 978-1-957213-07-1 (epub) | DOI: https://doi.org/10.21061/vt150
Subjects: PHOTOGRAPHY—History. | VIRGINIA POLYTECHNIC INSTITUTE AND STATE UNIVERSITY—History.

We dedicate this book to the countless researchers who visit our reading room and those who use our virtual research services to help better understand the history of Virginia Tech.

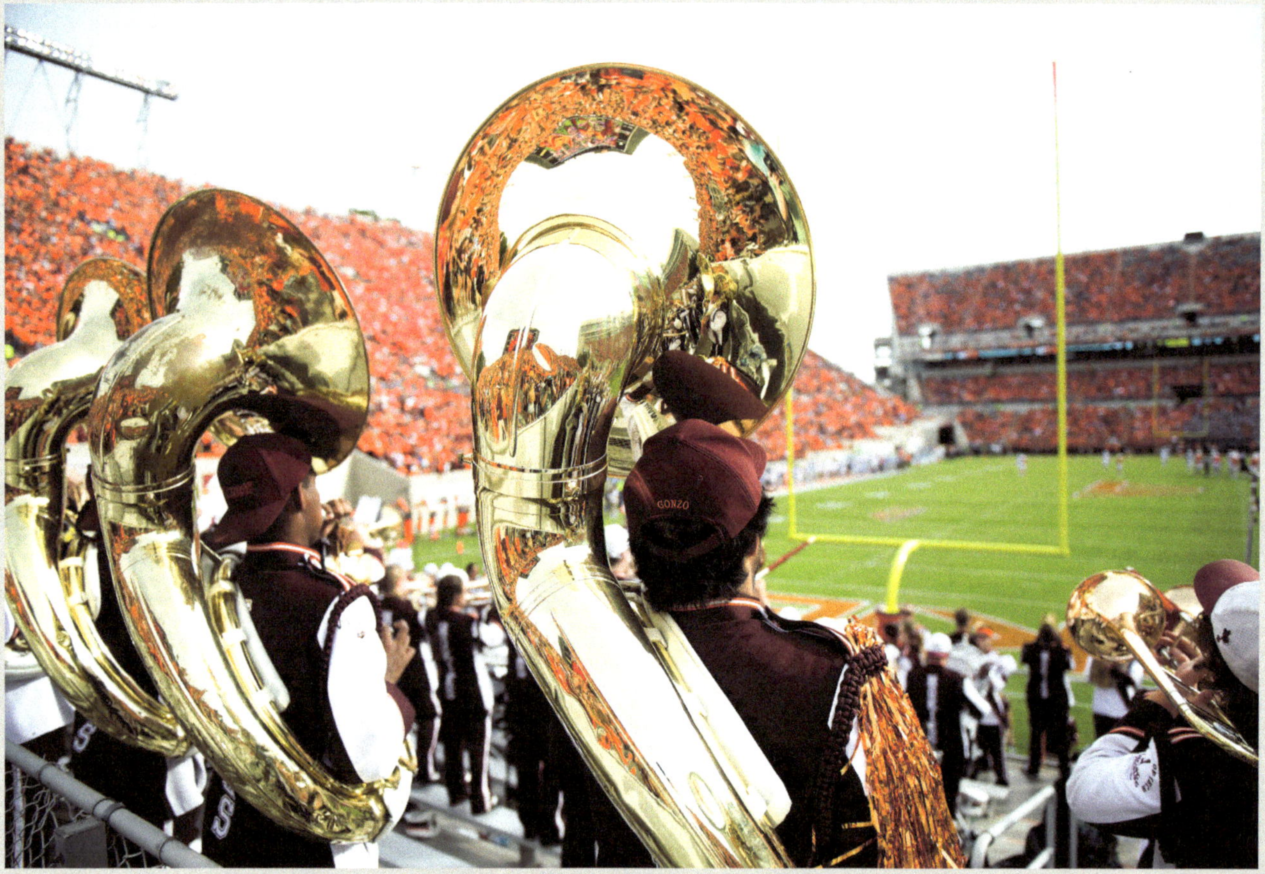
GONZO

CONTENTS

Preface ix
Acknowledgments xi

Introduction 1
PART 1: Land-Grant Mission 27
PART 2: Changing Campus 91
PART 3: Innovation 151

Further Reading 179
About the Authors 181
Index 183

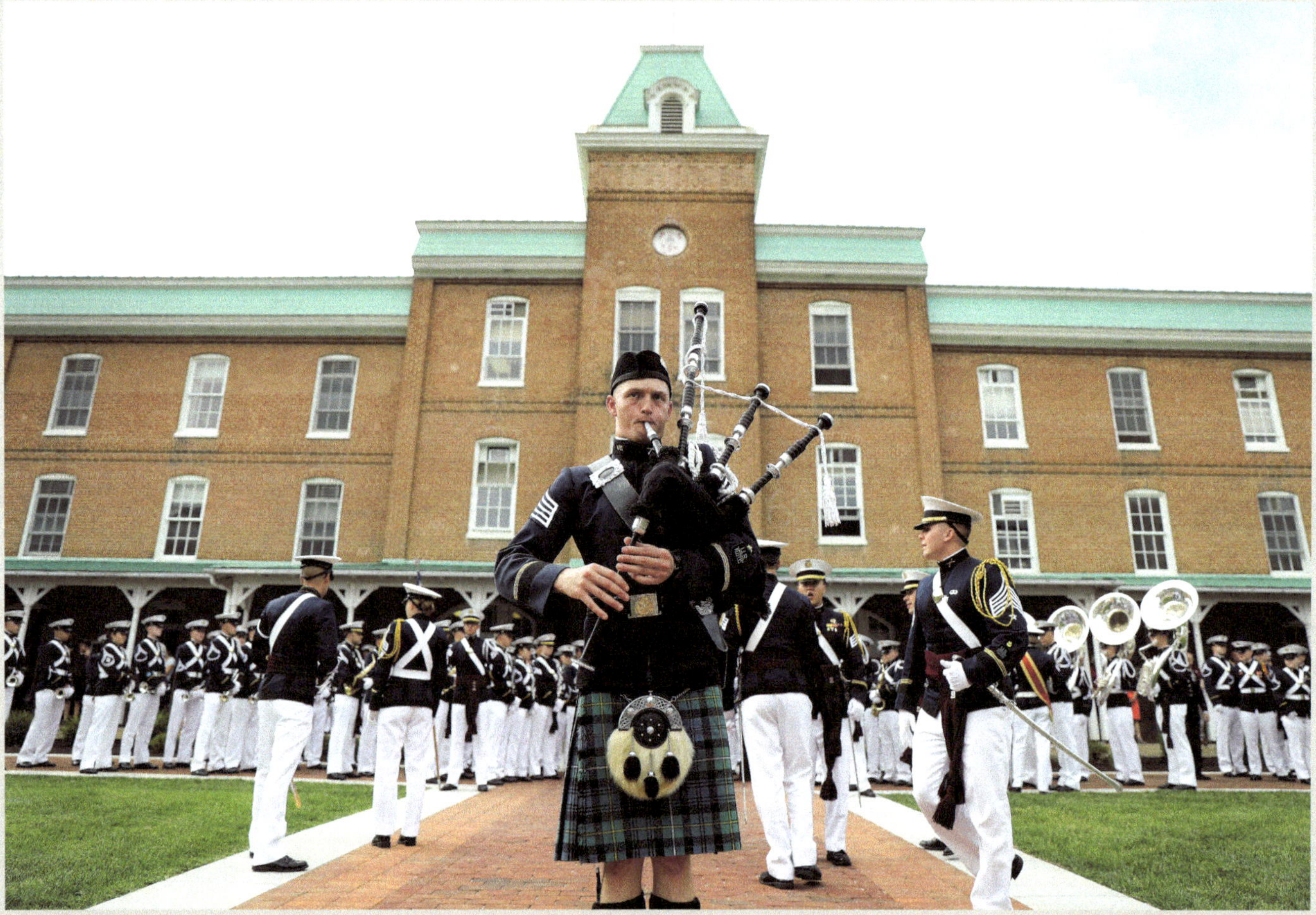

PREFACE

VIRGINIA TECH CELEBRATES its 150th anniversary in 2022. What started as a fledgling school established in Southwest Virginia to promote agricultural, mechanical, and military education grew into a comprehensive research university with a global land-grant mission. As part of the celebrations, *No Ordinary Moment: Virginia Tech, 150 Years in 150 Images* provides a unique look at the history of Virginia Polytechnic Institute and State University from its mid-nineteenth-century origins to the present day. The book features 150 illustrations (give or take a few), including numerous unique or rare photographs from the Special Collections and University Archives at Virginia Tech and other campus sources. These iconic and less-familiar historic photographs celebrate the milestones and lesser-known achievements of the past 150 years and point to the bright future of Virginia Tech.

Compiled and written by Virginia Tech archivists, *No Ordinary Moment* is organized around three principal themes—the land-grant mission, a changing campus, and a long tradition of innovation—which, taken together, provide an overlapping look at Virginia Tech's past, present, and future. Each section highlights the many notable milestones in the university's history, such as its founding as a land-grant college in 1872, the granting of university status in 1970, and the history of female students and students of color. Through illustrations and detailed captions, the book also illuminates the long-standing strengths of the university in the education of engineering, agriculture, architecture, and the sciences, as well as the athletics program and student activities. Also covered are the establishment of the Virginia Cooperative Extension and colleges for Medicine and Veterinary Medicine, and Virginia Tech's leading example in new technological fields and applied sciences, such as cybersecurity, transportation, autonomous vehicles, and bioinformatics.

We are grateful for the opportunity to celebrate 150 years of Virginia Tech's history. This books allows us to promote the holdings and services of Special Collections and University Archives at Virginia Tech. All proceeds received from the purchase of the book will be used to support Special Collections and University Archives at Virginia Tech. To all members of Hokie Nation, we hope you enjoy reading it as much as we enjoyed creating it!

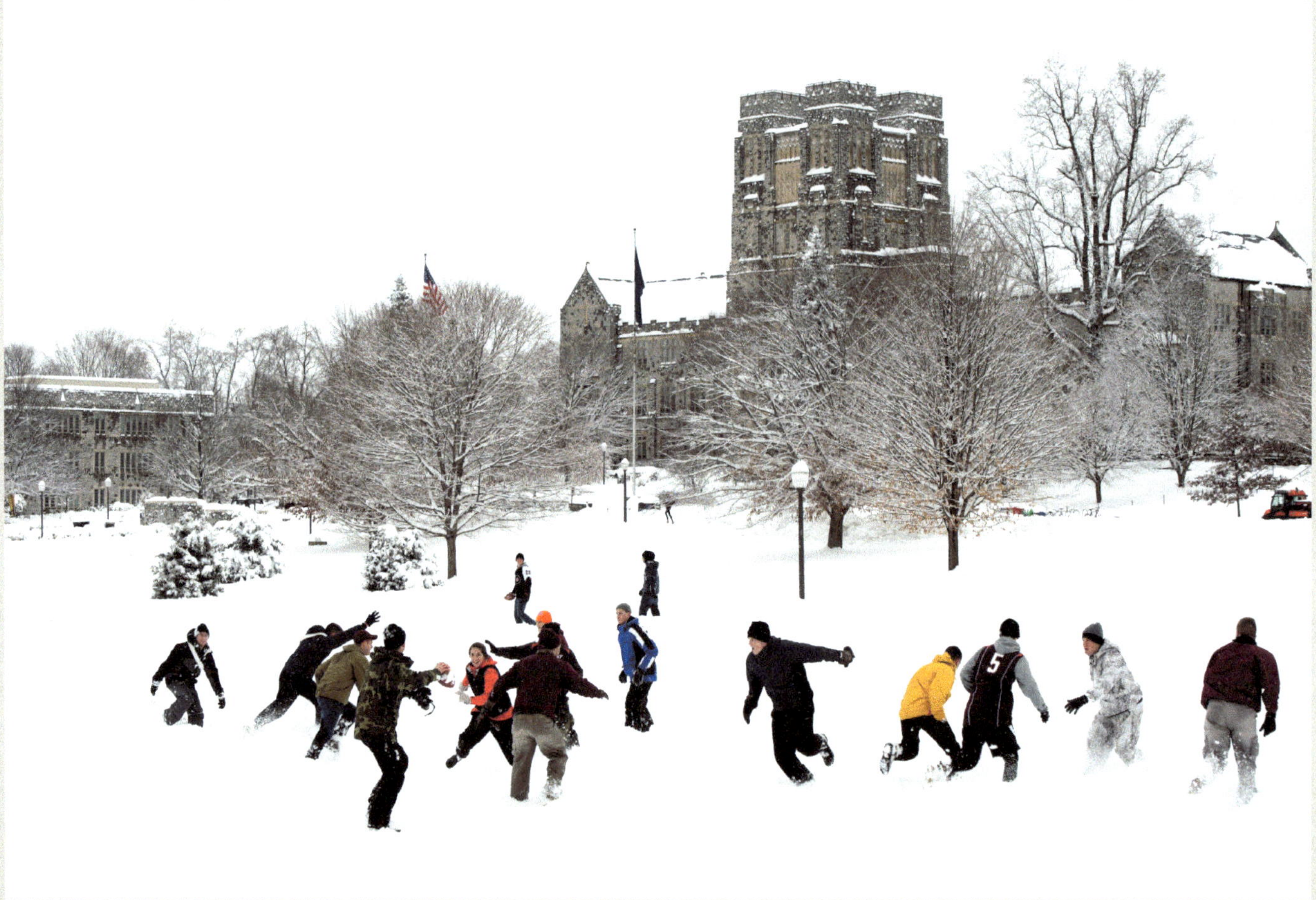

ACKNOWLEDGMENTS

THIS PROJECT BEGAN in the fall of 2019 as an idea hatched by four archivists in Special Collections and University Archives at Virginia Tech. We wanted to create a different type of book about Virginia Tech's history. Rather than a comprehensive historical account, we wanted something lighter and more visually striking, something that might draw upon—and draw attention to—the extraordinary wealth of historical materials in the University Archives. Plus, we all agreed that the book should address many of the gaps in the school's history, especially the students, events, and programs that have been historically neglected. We landed on the idea of a photographic journey that highlights both important and lesser-known achievements in the school's history. The theme of "no ordinary moment" served as the ideal vehicle for this journey, the phrase coming from Governor Walker's address at Virginia Agricultural and Mechanical College's first commencement exercises in July 1873.

Over the past two years, each person contributed to lengthy conversations about themes, content, selection, layout, publishers, audience, and timing. The four co-authors each focused on a specific part of the puzzle. Aaron D. Purcell compiled the introductory essay to introduce some of the highlights of the past 150 years. John M. Jackson tackled the first theme of the land-grant mission, which required him to find lesser-known images of many familiar topics in Virginia Tech's history. Anthony Wright de Hernandez organized content for the second theme of the changing campus. This portion included images related to events, people, and places that helped diversify and enrich the school. LM Rozema documented the third theme of innovation. The school has a long tradition of creative innovation, and this section shines a light on that tradition, with a particular focus on very recent times. It was a collaborative effort designed to share the rich collections of Special Collections and University Archives at Virginia Tech and other campus collections.

The authors wish to thank many supporters in the University Libraries for their support and insights. Most notably, Peter Potter, Director of Virginia Tech Publishing, was part of the project team and helped guide us through the publication process. Major funding for publication of this book came from the University Libraries and Virginia Tech's Sesquicentennial Steering Committee. The historical eyes of Clara Cox and Debbie Day, two experts on university history, were very much appreciated. University Relations and the Virginia Tech Athletic department helped us locate images to fill in the gaps. In addition, we would like to acknowledge the work of the following people who provided photographs and content—Mike Adamo, Mike Chirieleison, Olivia Coleman, Judy Davis, Mary Desmond, Christina Franusich, Rick Griffiths, Jason Jones, Rob Lyons, John McCormick, Ray Meese, Clayton Metz, Thomas Miller, Dan Mirolli, Althea Olinger, Chiravi Patel, Steve Tatum, Skyler Taube, Logan Wallace, Steven White, Ryan Young, and Megan Zalecki.

Finally, we would like to thank all of the supporters and employees of Special Collections and University Archives at Virginia Tech, past and present, for documenting, collecting, and preserving the university's history to make this book possible.

NO ORDINARY MOMENT

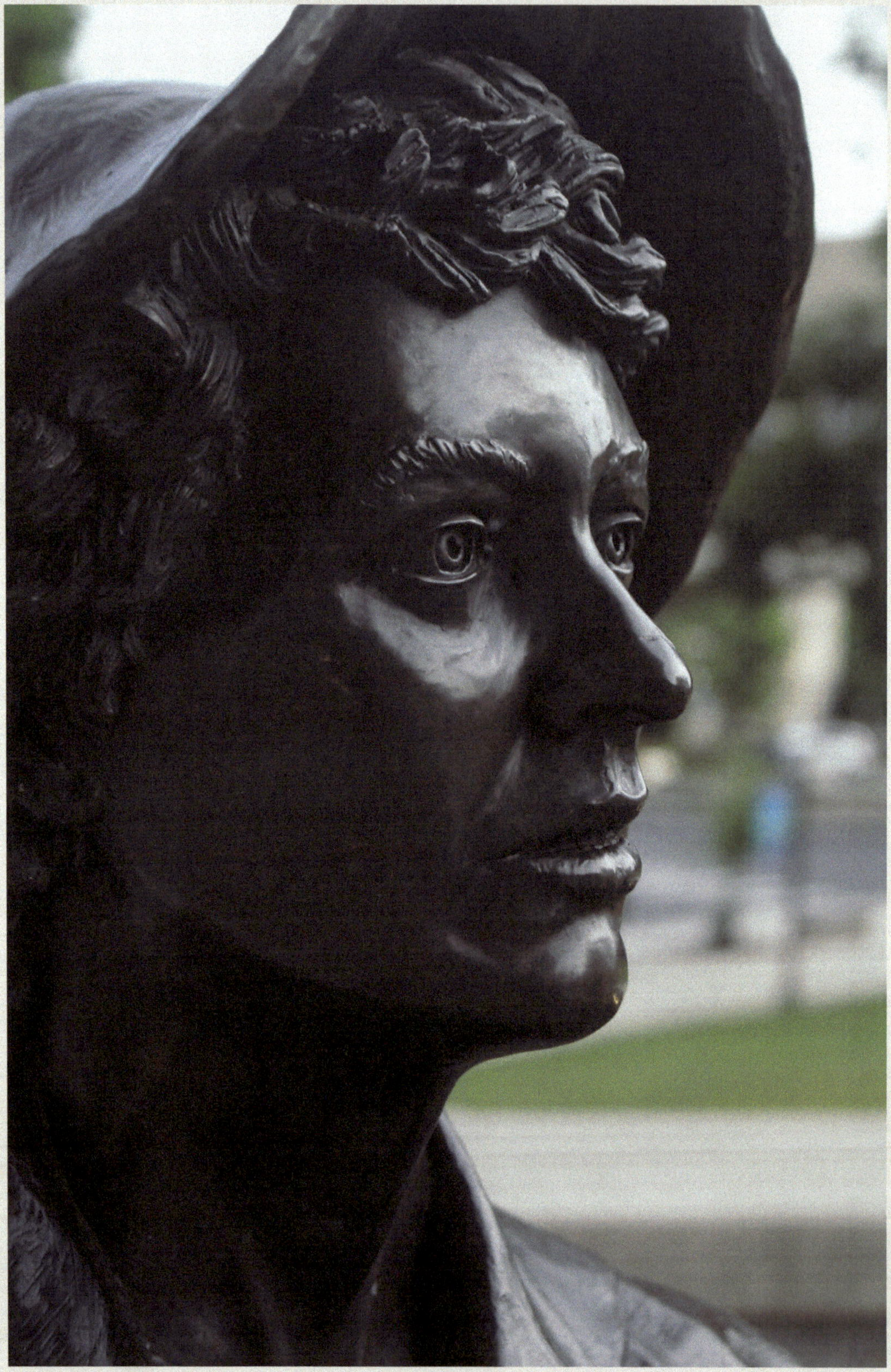

INTRODUCTION

WHAT'S IN A NAME? Virginia Tech, located in the mountains of Southwest Virginia, has taken on many names, both legal and popular, since it was first founded as a land-grant college in 1872—Virginia Agricultural and Mechanical College; Virginia Agricultural and Mechanical College and Polytechnic Institute; Virginia Polytechnic Institute; Virginia Polytechnic Institute and State University; and most commonly used today, Virginia Tech. But, of course, the school is more than a name. For many it represents a lengthy tradition of practical and affordable education, service (known by its motto *Ut Prosim*, Latin for That I May Serve), outreach, and a college experience like no other. Graduates, current students, and those who work at Virginia Tech often identify as Hokies, the name of the school's mascot.

The evolution of Virginia Tech over its 150 years mirrors many of the changes in higher education and culture since the late nineteenth century. But there are remarkable, difficult, and unique moments in the school's history that best explain why Virginia Tech is so important to so many people. This brief overview charts some of those milestones and places them in the context of Virginia Tech's broader history.

ORIGINS

All schools have their own origin story. Virginia Tech's story began with a contentious battle to designate a land-grant college in Virginia. The Morrill Act of 1862, signed into law by President Abraham Lincoln, provided grants of land to states to finance the establishment of a public institution of higher education in each state. Funding for these grants came from the public sale of lands in the West, which the federal government took from Indigenous peoples. Each state designated or created a new land-grant college. The purpose of these schools was to provide education focused on agriculture, engineering, and military training.

Like other Southern states that seceded from the United States during the Civil War, Virginia did not have access to land-grant funds until it was readmitted to the Union. Virginia returned to the Union in January 1870, months after enacting a new constitution and ratifying the 14th and 15th Amendments. This meant that Virginia was eligible to receive its share of the Morrill Act funds, but the new legislature was deeply divided over two important questions. The first was where to establish the new school. Some wanted the money to go to a well-established school (the University of Virginia and Virginia Military Institute were leading contenders) while others pushed for an entirely new institution, one created specifically to offer the kind of education envisioned in the Morrill Act. The second question was whether or not the funds should be divided between two schools—one for Black people and one for white people.

The General Assembly continued to debate these matters throughout the 1870 and 1871 sessions. Late in the game, a new contender entered the race: the Preston and Olin Institute in Blacksburg. A small Methodist school established in the 1850s, the Institute was struggling to survive when its trustees came up with the idea of offering the school to the state so that it could be turned into a land-grant school. To sweeten the deal, the residents of Montgomery County pledged $20,000—a substantial sum of money at the time—to fund the new school.

The land being offered up to the state has a rich and complex history. The Tutelo and Monacan peoples were the traditional custodians of the territory that today makes up much of Virginia and West Virginia. During the eighteenth century, the Preston family and other local families owned the land that would become Virginia Tech. This property included the Smithfield estate, the Solitude estate, and all the buildings of the Preston and Olin Institute. Between 40 and 100 enslaved African men, women, and children lived and worked at Smithfield. At Solitude, the number probably exceeded 30, including members of the Fraction family. In more recent times, Virginia Tech recognized the significance and contributions of both the Tutelo/Monacan peoples and the enslaved Africans and their descendants in making possible the founding of a major land-grant university.

Debate over the land-grant funding continued well into the 1872 legislative session. On March 19, 1872, Governor Gilbert C. Walker signed the bill that established the Virginia Agricultural and Mechanical College (VAMC) at Blacksburg. The legislation designated two-thirds of the land-grant funding to the education of white students, contingent on changing the name of the Preston and Olin Institute to the Virginia Agricultural and Mechanical College and turning over its property and buildings to the new school. The remaining one-third of the funding was given to Hampton Normal and Industrial Institute (and later to Virginia State University) for the education of Black people. The legislation also established that fees and tuition

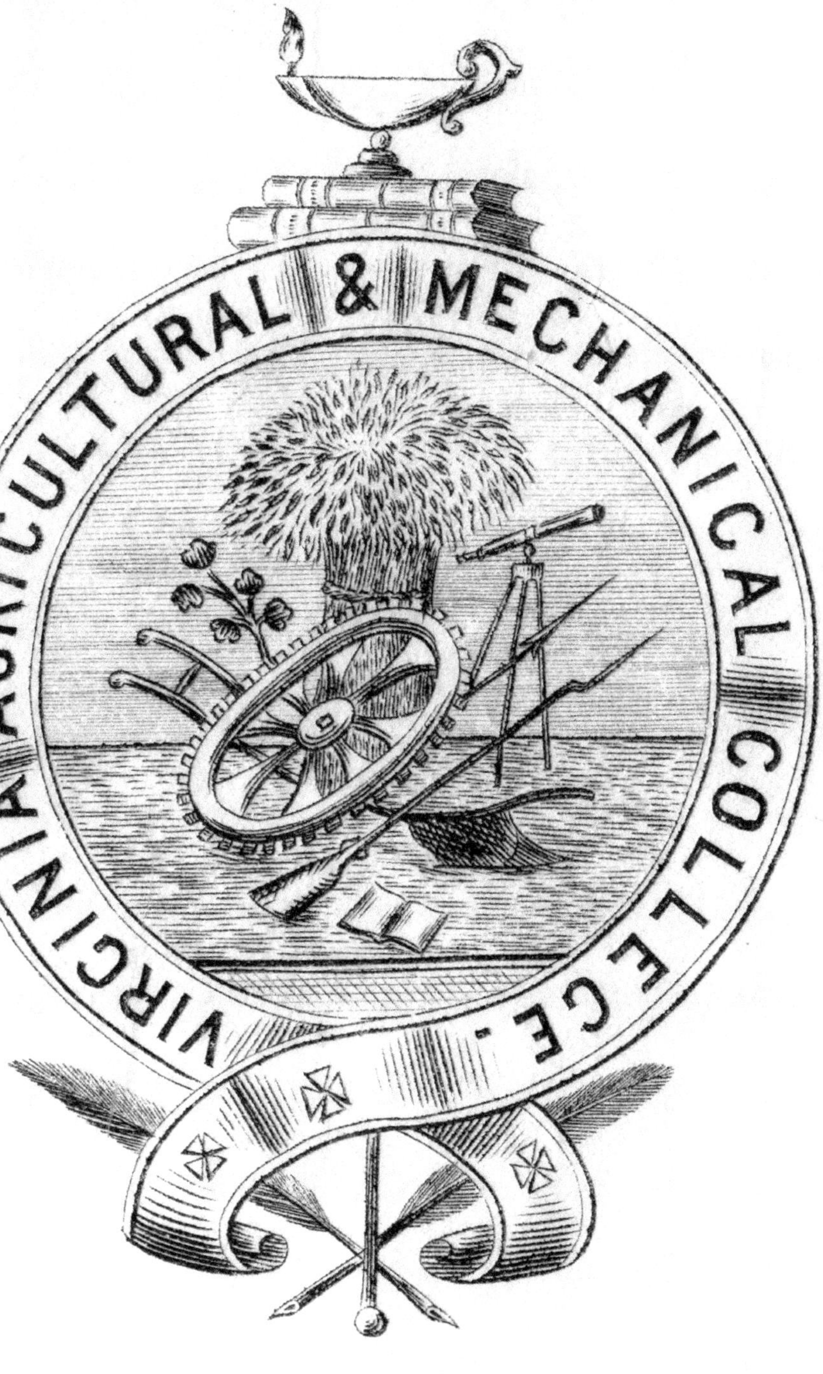
VIRGINIA AGRICULTURAL & MECHANICAL COLLEGE.

would be fully waived for the first admitted students, up to the number of members of the House of Delegates.

Governor Walker appointed a Board of Visitors, named because the group would not reside on campus, to guide the school. The board then hired a president and faculty, developed a curriculum, and finalized the purchase of the property and conveyance of the physical plant of the Preston and Olin Institute to the new school. Further, the board approved the purchase of the adjoining property and buildings of the Solitude estate. In carrying out these activities, the overarching goal of the board was to provide Virginians an inexpensive and practical education. Like the majority of colleges and universities established in the post-Civil War period, only white males were admitted.

The first curriculum was designed to be a three-year program resulting in a certificate for a specific area of study in either agriculture or mechanical arts. Students were to take a range of general courses in mathematics, English, geography, astronomy, penmanship, health and physiology, a foreign language (French or German), and government. Courses in engineering, agriculture, and military tactics (which required physically able students to participate in military training) matched the land-grant purpose. Students were also required to work on the farm or in workshops as part of their coursework.

During the summer of 1872, the Board of Visitors established fees for incoming students (around $200 tuition for an academic year) and hired key personnel including a handful of faculty to teach the first classes. During the board's third meeting in August 1872, the members held a vote to choose the school's first president. Out of several candidates, Charles Landon Carter Minor won narrowly—reportedly by a single vote.

Minor came to Blacksburg from Sewanee Episcopal Seminary in Tennessee, where he was then teaching Latin. He held a master of arts degree from the University of Virginia and had served previously as president of the Maryland Agricultural College (now the University of Maryland). During the Civil War, Minor served as a captain in the Confederacy. He saw action in several battles including the Battle of Bull Run. In fact, the first five presidents of VAMC (1872-1906) served as Confederate officers in the Civil War. This meant that, while the institution was founded after the Civil War, its early leadership was undoubtedly influenced by pro-Southern sentiment.

Virginia

Agricultural and Mechanical College

Blacksburg, Va. June 30th 1886.

Mr. **R. E. L. Aylor.**

Having successfully completed the prescribed Course of Study, is hereby declared a **GRADUATE** of this College, with the title of

Bachelor of Arts.

Thos. N. Conrad, President

Martin? Scott Prof. Agriculture & Nat. History

J. E. Christian, Prof. Mathematics

J. X. Morton, Prof. English & Latin

Floyd Davis, Prof. Chemistry & Metallurgy

[illegible] Prof. [illegible]

Wm. B. Graham, Prof. Book-Keeping &c.

Wm. E. Hubbel, Prof. Mod. Lang.

THE DOORS OPEN

On Tuesday, October 1, 1872, Virginia Agricultural and Mechanical College opened for business in Blacksburg. The first student to arrive was William Addison Caldwell, who came on foot from his family home in Craig County. The walk—20 to 28 miles depending on the route taken—is reenacted each year by the Corps of Cadets, who call it the "Caldwell March." By the end of the first week, only 29 students had arrived to begin courses. Discouraged by the low numbers and the notable disparity in the educational backgrounds of the new enrollees, Minor placed advertisements in regional newspapers for potential matriculates. The publicity worked. By the end of the 1872-1873 academic year, 132 young men from Virginia had enrolled at the new school.

VAMC's first commencement exercises were held in July 1873 with Governor Walker as the main speaker. It was too soon for the school to graduate students but the ceremony was a moment for celebration and reflection. Walker began his address by proclaiming, "The occasion of our assembling is one of no ordinary moment." The reason it was no ordinary moment was that it marked a new chapter in the history of Virginia. Walker said,

> Perhaps no event has transpired within our State for many years possessed of greater significance or of more far-reaching consequences than the organization of this Institution. For the first time in her history she has established a College primarily devoted to practical education.

GROWING PAINS

The most pressing challenge facing the fledgling college in those early years was a lack of funding to hire faculty and construct new buildings. The Preston and Olin Institute left behind only one building, which was woefully inadequate for the needs of educating and housing well over 100 young men. Requests for funding went unmet until 1875 when the General Assembly appropriated $45,000 for new buildings and an expansion of campus. But more challenges were to come.

From the start, military training was part of the curriculum, but the question of how much the school should be organized along military lines divided early leaders and faculty. Two factions emerged. Professor James H. Lane, who taught mathematics and foreign languages, wanted all students to live on campus and under military regulations. Lane, a graduate of Virginia Military Institute, was no doubt also reacting to growing tensions in town-gown relations resulting from the fact that most of the students at the time were living off campus and, suffice to say, not always behaving in ways that met the approval of townspeople. President Minor opposed Lane's strict dictates. Minor believed that the military drill required of all able-bodied students was sufficient. By the late 1870s, the disagreements between Lane and Minor had reached a breaking point. At a faculty meeting in March 1878, the two men got into a fistfight, which led to charges (and convictions) of disorderly conduct. After this incident, confidence in Minor's administration eroded, which ultimately resulted in the Board of Visitors removing him from office in late 1879 and replacing him in 1880 with John Lee Buchanan. Buchanan, who officially took office on March 1, 1880, quickly reorganized the curriculum to include mandatory military training, but both the requirement and his tenure were brief.

In the summer of 1880, the General Assembly stepped into the fray, declaring that VAMC was an agricultural and mechanical school, not a military academy. At the time, both houses were controlled by the short-lived Readjuster Party, which promised to reduce the Commonwealth's outstanding debt and invest in schools. They also replaced the school's Board of Visitors, advised the board to replace all faculty and officers, and hired and fired several presidents, including Buchanan a second time.

The subsequent decline of the Readjuster Party in Richmond during the 1880s resulted in further upheaval at VAMC. In 1882 Thomas Nelson Conrad was appointed the school's third president, thanks in large part to his ties to the Readjusters, but his time in office would be controversial. A former president of the Preston and Olin Institute, Conrad launched a reorganization plan that integrated military training into the curriculum and campus life. That shift meant that all students had to live on campus and participate in regular drill. During Conrad's tenure, a business department was added, and the school began offering an A.B. degree in the literary and scientific departments as well as degrees in civil engineering and mining engineering.

Also during Conrad's tenure, the board adopted a three-quarter—rather than two-semester—calendar for the academic year. This system, and the academic year, would change a number of times in the ensuing years. From 1905 to 1988 the school operated on a quarter system, but since that time Virginia Tech has followed a two-semester academic year.

Conrad's fortunes at VAMC declined with the waning of the Readjuster Party. As Democrats returned to power in Richmond, they sealed Conrad's fate. A new

Board of Visitors was created and met for the first time in March 1886, at which meeting they voted to remove all faculty and officers as of July 1, 1886. The board then selected a new president, Lunsford Lindsay Lomax, who started on Conrad's last day. Another ex-Confederate general, Lomax was farming in Fauquier County at the time of his appointment and had little relevant experience to recommend him for such a position. His presidency was relatively brief (1886-1891) but it saw a few notable developments. The legislature designated funds to construct Barracks No. 1, known today as Lane Hall. The new building housed all of the cadets and marked the beginning of the development of the Upper Quad portion of campus. In 1888 the school accepted federal funds from the Hatch Act of 1887 to establish an Agricultural Experiment Station on nearly 250 acres on land about half a mile outside of Blacksburg.

Lomax was forced to resign as president in 1891 following an embarrassing incident—a student party that got out of control, leading to considerable damage to Barracks No. 1. In his place, the Board of Visitors appointed John McLaren McBryde as the school's fifth president. McBryde, a graduate of the University of Virginia and, like his predecessors, a former Confederate officer, brought to the job experience as a professor of agriculture and botany at the University of Tennessee and as president of South Carolina College.

REORGANIZING FOR A NEW CENTURY

During his 16 years as president, McBryde transformed the struggling land-grant school into a modern twentieth-century college. In fact, McBryde's reorganization plan was the foundation of modern-day Virginia Tech. He proposed that the land-grant school become more professional and technical and called for seven four-year courses that would lead to bachelor of science degrees and for two shorter courses that would lead to certificates, all falling under either agriculture or mechanics, which later in his administration was called engineering. The Board of Visitors approved the ambitious plan and allowed McBryde to reshape nearly every aspect of the school.

Among the many highlights of McBryde's presidency were the expansion of the physical plant and the building of dormitories and faculty houses; the use of "Hokie Stone" (a local limestone) in new buildings; the planting of more than 2,000 ornamental trees on campus; and construction of "The Grove," a residence for the president. In academics, McBryde was responsible for adding seven new bachelor of science degree programs as well as graduate programs. During his tenure, the college was divided into departments, each with its own faculty and dean. He also created a dean of the faculty position, and appointed a career military officer as commandant. While all this was happening, the size of the faculty increased dramatically, from 9 in 1891 to 48 by 1907, and the college constructed new housing in what became known as Faculty Row.

Another important, if symbolic, change came during McBryde's presidency. In 1896, to better reflect the combined programs of agriculture, mechanics, and scientific technology, the General Assembly changed the school's name to Virginia Agricultural and Mechanical College and Polytechnic Institute. As this was a mouthful, it was quickly shortened in popular usage to Virginia Polytechnic Institute, or VPI. In 1944 the name of the school would officially change to Virginia Polytechnic Institute.

Student life flourished during McBryde's tenure. Student enrollment grew from 135 in 1891 to a peak of 728 in 1904-1905. There were a number of significant "firsts" during this period including new athletic teams and sports, the first campus newspaper, the publication of a yearbook called the *Bugle*, the adoption of Chicago maroon and burnt orange as school colors, and creation of a new seal. In addition, *Ut Prosim* became the official school motto.

Also during this period, "Hokie" became one of the nicknames for the students. In 1896, the addition of "and Polytechnic Institute" to the school's name facilitated the need for a new cheer to replace "Rip! Rah! Ree! Va! Va! Vee! Virginia, Virginia, A. M. C.!" The Athletic Association held a contest with a $5 prize to pick a new cheer. O. M. Stull, Class of 1896, won the contest with his spirit cheer, now known as "Old Hokie." The original went:

Hoki, Hoki, Hoki, Hy.
Techs, Techs, V.P.I.
Sola-Rex, Sola-Rah.
Polytechs - Vir-gin-ia.
Rae, Ri, V.P.I.

An "e" was later added to "Hoki" to make "Hokie," and "Team! Team! Team!" was attached to the end.

In late 1906 McBryde announced his resignation due to poor health. In January 1907 the Board of Visitors elected him president emeritus and conferred upon him the honorary degree of Doctor of Science, the first such honor ever accorded by the college.

WARTIME AND EXPANSION

Like other land-grant universities, Virginia Polytechnic Institute changed significantly during the first decades of the twentieth century. In response to the need for more farmers, better agricultural practices, and sharing information with rural communities, the school launched extension, outreach, and demonstration programs.

Two notable figures during these years were Ella Graham Agnew and Thomas O. Sandy. Beginning in 1914, when extension services moved to VPI, Agnew led the college's extension service. This was, of course, before VPI admitted women to study. A resident of Prince Edward County, Agnew became the nation's first home demonstration agent.

Thomas O. Sandy, from Essex County, was Virginia's first agricultural extension agent. He opened an extension office in Burkeville in 1907. In the 1910s Sandy led VPI's agricultural extension programs across Virginia. Through extension and demonstration programs, Virginia Tech made a connection to every county in Virginia. In the next decade, a group of Virginia Tech professors organized the Future

RECREATION FIELD

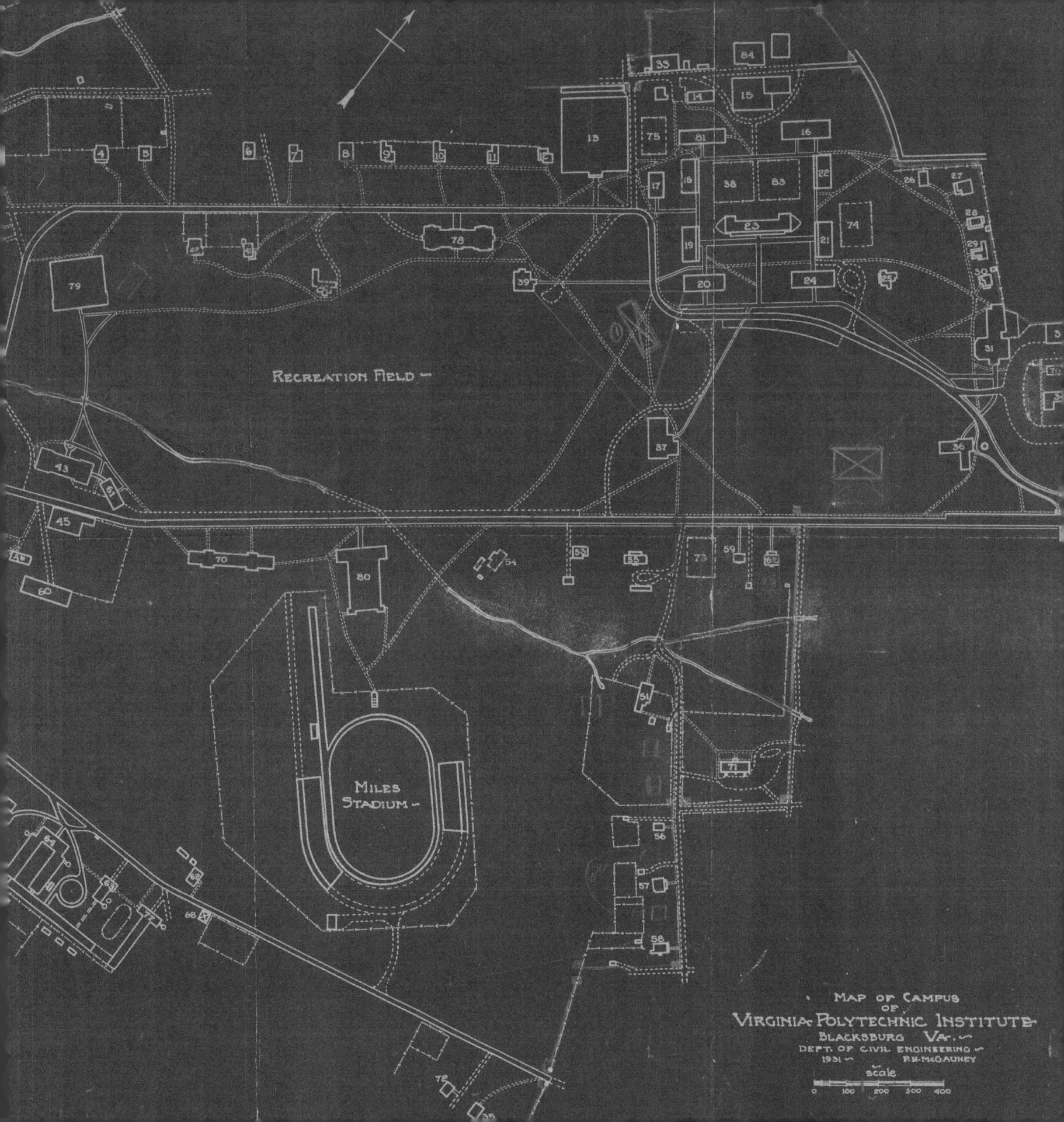

MILES STADIUM

MAP OF CAMPUS
OF
VIRGINIA POLYTECHNIC INSTITUTE
BLACKSBURG VA.
DEPT. OF CIVIL ENGINEERING
1931 — R.H. McGAUHEY
scale
0 100 200 300 400

Farmers of Virginia, which soon became the model for a new nationwide organization, the Future Farmers of America.

The United States entered World War I in April 1917. VPI responded by operating a 12-month training school for the Army and the Navy. Large numbers of VPI students joined the armed forces. In total, over 2,200 VPI alumni served in World War I, which represented 43 percent of the alumni up to that point. The military recognized many VPI students for their bravery, including Earle D. Gregory, who became the first Virginian to receive the nation's Medal of Honor. Twenty-six VPI students died in battle or while in training. In 1926, VPI dedicated the War Memorial Gymnasium to the VPI servicemen who sacrificed their lives in World War I.

In the closing days of World War I, Julian A. Burruss became the eighth president of VPI. Unlike his predecessors, Burruss was a VPI alumnus (1898), held a Ph.D. (University of Chicago), and had experience leading a women's college (the Normal and Industrial School for Women in Harrisonburg, now James Madison University). Burruss was a transformative president and led the school for more than a quarter century. During his presidency, VPI's physical plant grew to include more barracks in the historic part of campus and development of the campus to the west. The Drillfield and many of the iconic buildings visible from it were built during the 1920s and 1930s. Also in 1923, Burruss modified the mandatory four-year military requirement for male students to two years, making the last two years optional. Among Burruss's many accomplishments, perhaps his most significant was to persuade the Board of Visitors to admit women to VPI. The college had accepted part-time women students in agriculture-related summer courses as early as 1913 or 1914, but in 1921, to mixed responses from the campus and alumni communities, the first full-time women students enrolled at Virginia Tech. Mary E. Brumfield, Billie Kent Kabrich, Lucy Lee Lancaster, Carrie T. Sibold, and Ruth Louise Terrett forever changed Virginia Tech. They enrolled in academic programs such as biology, chemistry, and civil engineering. In 1923, Mary Brumfield became the first woman to graduate, and in 1925 she became the first to earn a master's degree.

Because the cadets excluded them from most of the campus organizations and the yearbook, women students developed their own activities and spheres of influence. For example, women students published the *Tin Horn*, a yearbook for female students in 1925, 1929, 1930, and 1931, and organized a Women's Student Organization. Coeds were exempt from service, and the cadet corps did not allow women to join until over 50 years later. Initially, women students had to live at home, if their families were nearby, or had to board in town. Later, the college designated a few existing dormitories and other buildings for women. Hillcrest Hall, built in 1940, was the first new dormitory on campus built specifically for women students. As they made their mark on VPI, women students became more integrated into campus life. Women had been on the staff at VPI since the early 1900s, but the first woman faculty member, Anna Campbell, started in 1922, the year before the first five coeds matriculated.

WORLD WAR II AND COMMEMORATION

The United States officially entered World War II in December 1941 after the bombing of Pearl Harbor. Students enlisted and employees left for positions in wartime industries, especially the nearby Radford Ordnance Works. The student body declined from a high of 3,582 in 1942-1943 to a low of 738 in 1944-1945. Altogether, more than 7,000 VPI students served in the armed forces during the war. Over 300 of those students died; 3 received the Medal of Honor, 2 posthumously. The college operated several special war training programs, including the Army Specialized Training Program, used primarily for Army engineers. At the peak of the war, these war training programs brought as many as 2,000 soldiers to the campus.

After the end of the war in 1945, VPI commemorated the service of students and alumni by constructing the War Memorial Chapel on the east end of the Drillfield. Completed in 1960, the chapel has a number of distinctive features. The upper level, known as Memorial Court, contains eight sculptured Indiana limestone pylons representing brotherhood, honor, leadership, sacrifice, service, loyalty, duty, and *Ut Prosim*. The names of all Hokies who sacrificed their lives during military service are etched into the pylons. A marble cenotaph, centered at the back of Memorial Court, includes the etched names of the seven alumni awarded the Medal of Honor. The lower level contains a 6,324-square-foot, 260-seat chapel, which, in addition to being a place for religious services and other commemorative events, has been a favorite site over the years for weddings.

POSTWAR DIVERSITY

Coeducation took a major step forward in Virginia during the 1940s as the war led to a decline in the male student population. Governor Colgate W. Darden Jr. (1942-1946) advocated for expansion of coeducation through consolidation. In 1944 he engineered the merger of VPI and nearby Radford College, in an arrangement similar to that between the University of Virginia and Mary Washington College. Radford's new name became Radford College, Women's Division of Virginia Polytechnic Institute. Women could still take classes at the Blacksburg campus, but only in the core areas of engineering, agriculture, or business. Teacher training programs were centralized at the Radford location. The first two years of home economics studies were held at Radford, while the final two years were at Blacksburg. The arrangement proved problematic as many coeds had to ride buses between the campuses to complete their academic programs.

The return of veterans after World War II led to a spike in enrollment at VPI. With support from the G.I. Bill, incoming students flooded both the Blacksburg and Radford campuses. Like other land-grant universities, VPI erected trailer parks to house students and secured temporary buildings for classrooms. Enrollment peaked at 5,458 in the 1947-1948 school year. The new students outnumbered returning students and most of the new enrollees registered as civilians, not members of the Corps of Cadets.

VPI's student body became increasingly international and diverse over the course of the twentieth century, although it was by no means a steady process. The first international student, James Dunsmuir of British Columbia, Canada, enrolled at

VAMC in 1874. The first Asian graduate was Cato Lee, from Hong Kong, who completed his degree work in mechanical engineering in 1927. After World War II, more international students enrolled at VPI, but Black people had a difficult time gaining entrance. Since the 1880s, small numbers of Black people had worked on campus, but VPI did not admit them as students until the 1950s. In 1953, a year before the landmark Supreme Court decision in *Brown* v *Board of Education of Topeka*, VPI admitted Irving L. Peddrew III, the school's first Black student. On one hand, VPI's admission of Peddrew represented an important milestone—VPI became the first public Southern university to admit a Black undergraduate. On the other hand, VPI intended to admit only a few Black students each year and to keep their collegiate experience separate from white students. Peddrew, who wanted to study electrical engineering, was required to live and eat off campus. This type of segregation continued into the late 1950s. The first Black student to earn a degree was Charlie L. Yates in 1958. In the fall of 1966 Linda Adams, Jacquelyn Butler, Linda Edmonds, LaVerne Hairston, Marguerite Harper, and Chiquita Hudson became the first Black women to matriculate at Virginia Tech. During the late 1960s, VPI hired its first Black faculty members and awarded degrees to its first female Black students. By the late 1960s,

Black students became more common on campus and more integrated into student life. Indigenous students matriculated at Virginia Tech throughout the mid-twentieth century. In 2007 Rufus Elliott became Virginia Tech's first Monacan student to graduate, an important milestone for the university in serving the people on whose traditional land the institution sits.

TRANSFORMATIVE FIGURE

In 1962 the VPI Board of Visitors appointed T. Marshall Hahn, a physicist, businessman, and academic leader, as the eleventh president. During his dozen years in office, 1962-1974, Hahn transformed a technically oriented college into a comprehensive research university. He did so by expanding the school's academic offerings and programs, improving the physical plant, and increasing and diversifying the student body—all during a tumultuous period of student unrest and unparalleled growth.

Hahn's influence on VPI is hard to overstate. He first renamed all existing "schools," except the graduate school, as "colleges," which included the colleges of engineering, agriculture, business, home economics, architecture, and arts and sciences. He added new undergraduate programs in the humanities and the arts, a teacher training program, and new doctoral programs in the sciences. To encourage greater enrollment, Hahn abolished the mandatory military requirement for all male freshmen and sophomores. In 1964, with strong support from Hahn, the state legislature confirmed the separation of VPI from Radford College, which was at the time the largest college for women in the state. The demerger allowed VPI to become fully coeducational. Hahn kept his pledge to improve outreach and extension services by constructing several new off-campus research stations. The president also embarked on an aggressive effort to increase faculty salaries and recruit nationally known faculty. In 1966 alone, more than 100 new faculty with doctorates joined VPI.

Hahn prepared VPI for baby boomers. He called for the construction of new dormitories, research laboratories, and athletic facilities, as well as an expansion of the school's airport. VPI's Board of Visitors approved his recommendations to add new programs of study in fields such as engineering, nuclear science, business, computer science, biochemistry, theatre arts, and philosophy. To better coordinate academic and statewide programs, Hahn created two new institution-wide divisions, one for research and one for extension. In addition, he successfully advocated for a statewide system of community colleges to open up higher education to many more Virginians. By 1967 VPI's enrollment topped 12,000 students, more than double the highest figure prior to his presidency. In 1970, to better reflect the school's growth and expanded role, the General Assembly renamed VPI as the Virginia Polytechnic Institute and State University. The name was later shortened to Virginia Tech.

The school's growth and the national political climate of the period brought immediate challenges to the institution. Cadets, who had adopted a constitution for student government in 1908, merged with the Civilian Student Body to form the Unified Student Body (later the Student Government Association and now the Undergraduate Student Senate) in 1966, but many students demanded greater involvement in university governance. Other national issues of the period, including protests against the Vietnam War, led to a few demonstrations on campus. The killing of four students by national guardsmen at Kent State University on May 4, 1970, led to the most significant student protest. On May 12, 1970, more than 100 students occupied Williams Hall. Hahn quickly ended the standoff by ordering state police to arrest the protesters and, upon their arrest, Hahn temporarily suspended all of them.

MILESTONES

Virginia Tech marked its centennial in 1972. Various centennial events took place, including Founders Day on March 24, 1972, which included descendants of the first student's family, first Board of Visitors, and various presidents. Concurrently, Montgomery County celebrated the centennial of the county's pledge of $20,000 to help launch the school.

Two years later, T. Marshall Hahn resigned as president. During his tenure, the school constructed 25 new buildings and added numerous fields of study, including 30 undergraduate programs. Under Hahn's guidance, the school became a nationally known research university. The VPI Board of Visitors named him president emeritus in 1975. In recognition of his accomplishments and his family's ongoing contributions, four buildings on Virginia Tech's Blacksburg campus bear the Hahn name.

A RESEARCH UNIVERSITY WITH NATIONAL ACCLAIM

By the 1980s Virginia Tech, like other public land-grant universities, was increasingly focused on research. In 1987 the school entered the list of the nation's top 50 research universities. Part of this growth came from the development of the Corporate Research Center (CRC) near the airport. Through the CRC, Virginia Tech forged partnerships with private companies, startups, and research initiatives supported by external grants. At the same time, Virginia Tech renewed its commitment to undergraduate education, recruitment of Virginia students, and community outreach through a new Public Services Division (later Outreach and International Development).

The growth of the school also brought unforeseen challenges and controversies. In 1986 President William Edward Lavery (1975-1987) approved an exchange of 247 acres of land (part of which became the site for a central shopping district in nearby Christiansburg) for 1,700 acres of farmland (known as Kentland) needed for agricultural research. Former Virginia Tech employees and benefactors were involved in the questionable exchange, and the press criticized the school's handling of what was dubbed as the "land swap."

The 1990s saw Virginia Tech further expand its reach, both in the state and beyond. In 1993 the university partnered with the City of Roanoke in a joint multi-million-dollar restoration and remodeling renovation of the Hotel Roanoke, which became the Hotel Roanoke and Conference Center, and the Northern Virginia Center in Falls Church. Efforts to construct a highway between Blacksburg and Roanoke during this period resulted in the Smart Road, where various transportation technologies such as autonomous vehicles are tested for the Virginia Tech Transportation Institute. In 1993 Virginia Tech, the Town of Blacksburg, and the C&P Telephone Company launched the Blacksburg Electronic Village. This project created an online community linking the entire town long before wireless networks existed. In 1992 the university, through the Virginia Tech Foundation, purchased an eighteenth-century villa known as Villa Maderni in Riva San Vitale, Switzerland, as a living and learning space for Virginia Tech students. In 2014 the building was renamed the Steger Center for International Scholarship.

Virginia Tech promoted the use of technology in the classroom through the Faculty Development Initiative (now known as the Professional Development Network), which provided technology training for faculty members. For students, the university created the Math Emporium, a giant computer lab offering self-paced mathematics courses. Since 1996 all graduate students have submitted their theses or dissertations in electronic format, making Virginia Tech the first school to require Electronic Theses and Dissertations (ETDs). Virginia Tech also developed Network Virginia, a broad bandwidth network, for the commonwealth. At the end of the twentieth century, the number of online courses available through Virginia Tech skyrocketed.

For many, Virginia Tech represents consistently competitive athletic programs. Once known as the Fighting Gobblers, the Hokies (and the HokieBird mascot) gained national notoriety during the last three decades of the twentieth century. The men's basketball team won the National Invitational Tournament championship in 1973 and 1995, and the women's basketball team won conference championships in

1994 and 1998. Both teams frequently participate in the NCAA tournament. Virginia Tech's football team gained the most attention during the coaching career of Frank Beamer, 1987–2015. He led the Hokies to 23 straight bowl game appearances, with the 2000 Sugar Bowl national championship game as the most notable; won seven conference championship titles; and was instrumental in moving Virginia Tech into the Atlantic Coast Conference (ACC) in 2004. Other varsity sports compete nationally and the school sponsors a variety of intramural athletic programs for students.

HEALTH EDUCATION

In the early 2000s Virginia Tech expanded its programs in the fields of veterinary medicine, health sciences, and medical research. The Virginia-Maryland College of Veterinary Medicine began as a partnership in 1979 between Virginia and Maryland to offer a regional approach to preparing veterinarians. The college, located in Blacksburg, opened a $10.5 million Infectious Disease Research Facility in November 2011 and completed a $14.1 million Veterinary Medicine Instruction Addition in the fall of 2012. In 2003 Virginia Tech and Wake Forest University formed a partnership to create a School of Biomedical Engineering and Sciences. The program offers graduate degrees in biomedical engineering. Related research and academic support comes from the Fralin Life Sciences Institute at Virginia Tech in Blacksburg. First formed in August 2008, the Fralin Life Sciences Institute includes the Fralin Biotechnology Center, the Institute for Biomedical and Public Health Sciences, and the Biocomplexity Institute.

In 2001 the Edward Via College of Osteopathic Medicine admitted its first students. Created in partnership with Virginia Tech and located in Blacksburg, this private osteopathic medical school offers medical training for students in Appalachia. Branch campuses later opened in South Carolina, Alabama, and Louisiana, which makes the school the second largest osteopathic medical school in the country. In 2007 Virginia Tech announced a public-private partnership with Carilion Clinic, a health care organization based in Roanoke. The resulting campus in Roanoke houses the Virginia Tech Carilion School of Medicine and the Fralin Biomedical Research Institute. In 2018 the VTC School of Medicine became Virginia Tech's ninth college.

PRINCIPLES OF COMMUNITY

At the beginning of the twenty-first century, a number of groups at Virginia Tech advocated for a stronger commitment to inclusion and diversity. This effort to improve the overall campus climate became part of strategic planning and was integrated into teaching, learning, and working at Virginia Tech. As a reflection of Virginia Tech's commitment to creating an inclusive and diverse community, in March 2005 the Board of Visitors endorsed the "Virginia Tech Principles of Community." This document affirms the dignity and value of every person, the right to express opinions freely within a climate of civility and mutual respect, the value of diversity, and our common humanity despite our differences. The principles reject all forms of prejudice and discrimination, encourage individual and collective responsibility for helping to eliminate bias and discrimination, and pledge to deepen our awareness of these challenges. In 2014 the Board of Visitors reaffirmed Virginia Tech's commitment to the "Principles of Community." The Board of Visitors acknowledges that bias and exclusion are part of the school's legacy, but the shared principles were fundamental to ongoing efforts to increase access and inclusion and to create a community that nurtures learning and growth for all of its members.

APRIL 16, 2007

On April 16, 2007, a mentally unstable Virginia Tech student murdered 32 students and faculty members on the Blacksburg campus before killing himself. It remains the deadliest school shooting in U.S. history. Spontaneous memorials appeared on the campus to commemorate the dead. In the days and weeks after the tragedy, Virginia Tech received condolences from tens of thousands of individuals and groups. The University Libraries collected over 500 linear feet of condolence material. In July 2007 the university created an Office of Recovery and Support to make resources available to the families of the victims, the physically injured and their families, and others directly affected by the tragedy. The event attracted international attention and elevated discussions about mental health and gun culture. Critics, including many of the victims' families, believed that the university's administration did not respond fast enough to warn students of the danger after the shooter murdered two students in a residence hall. The killings recommenced about two hours later in a classroom on the opposite side of campus. A series of lawsuits against Virginia Tech resulted in settlements with many of the victims' families. Each year, Virginia Tech coordinates commemoration events in mid-April to remember the 32 Hokies who died on April 16, 2007, including the signature 3.2-mile Run in Remembrance event that draws over 10,000 participants annually.

THE ARTS AND INNOVATION

In the first decades of the twenty-first century, Virginia Tech continued its commitment to integrating technology into the lives of students, faculty, staff, and all Hokies. In 2013 the Moss Arts Center opened its doors to support the performing arts. The building, located on the Alumni Mall, includes a 1,260-seat performance hall, visual arts galleries, amphitheater, the Cube (a four-story-high, state-of-the-art theatre and high-tech laboratory), and multiple studios. The Moss Arts Center is part of a larger Creativity and Innovation District (CID) on the eastern edge of campus. The

CID supports a new residential living experience known as Living-Learning Communities.

In the 2010s Virginia Tech embarked on a bold vision of the future known as Beyond Boundaries. As part of this initiative, the university established Destination Areas (DAs) to address complex and critical problems affecting the human condition across disciplines and communities. The DAs are intended to combine existing academic and research strengths with innovative transdisciplinary teams, tools, and processes. In 2018 Virginia Tech announced a $1 billion investment in building an Innovation Campus in Northern Virginia. Located in Alexandria, and near Amazon's planned HQ2 facility in Crystal City, the Innovation Campus will support graduate programs in computer science and computer engineering.

Virginia Tech played a crucial role in the development of drone delivery and research. In 2016 Wing, an offshoot of Google's parent company Alphabet, partnered with the Virginia Tech Mid-Atlantic Aviation Partnership (MAAP) to begin testing drone delivery. In October 2019, the partners conducted the first residential commercial drone delivery program in the United States. The use of drones at Virginia Tech is not limited to researchers or industry leaders. In 2018 Virginia Tech opened an outdoor Drone Park intended primarily for student and faculty use. At 85 feet tall, the Drone Park is the largest of its kind in the United States.

COVID-19

Beginning in March 2020, Virginia Tech responded to the COVID-19 global pandemic by transitioning to online education and limiting access to campus facilities. As face coverings became the new normal, Virginia Tech students, faculty, and staff adjusted to the restrictions. In the fall of 2020, students were allowed to return to campus, but many did not because the majority of courses were offered online. In late spring 2021, vaccines became available for Virginia Tech employees. Students returned to a relatively normal campus experience in the fall of 2021. Throughout the pandemic faculty and researchers at Virginia Tech made numerous contributions to public health, including processing over 100,000 COVID-19 tests in the Molecular Diagnostics Laboratory and conducting aerosol transmission research.

LOOKING BACK AT 150 YEARS

In 2017 President Timothy D. Sands appointed a 25-member Council on Virginia Tech History. He charged the group with exploring how Virginia Tech might recognize and acknowledge its history in the context of today and the future as the school prepares for its 150th anniversary in 2022. The council developed a number of innovative projects and programs for the 150th anniversary, many of which point to the contributions of previously underrepresented and historically marginalized communities. In 2022 a number of campus groups and organizers will coordinate a year-long series of events to mark Virginia Tech's founding 150 years ago.

The Council on Virginia Tech History also played an important role in reevaluating Virginia Tech's difficult and contested past. In the summer of 2020, President Sands asked the council to reexamine the names of specific buildings on campus. As background, during the preparations for Virginia Tech's 125th anniversary in 1997, students in a history class came across entries in the 1896 *Bugle*, presenting Claudius Lee as a member of racist organizations on campus. In response, the university formed a committee to investigate whether to rename Lee Hall. The committee report, issued in 1997, stated that the yearbook pages were distasteful jokes and concluded that the hall would not be renamed at that time. Twenty-three years later, during the summer of 2020, the issue resurfaced during national discourse on the subject of racism following the deaths of George Floyd, Breonna Taylor, and Ahmaud Arbery. In response to a new evaluation by the council, Virginia Tech renamed both Lee Hall and Barringer Hall as Hoge Hall and Whitehurst Hall, respectively. The university chose the new names to honor the Hoge family who housed Virginia Tech's first Black students before they were permitted to live on campus, and James Leslie Whitehurst Jr., the first Black student permitted to live on campus.

From its founding as the state's land-grant institution in 1872, Virginia Tech has committed itself to providing practical education through innovative methods. Virginia Tech leaders, students, faculty, staff, and alumni have shaped its history, experienced its highs and lows, and emphasized the commitment to service embodied in the motto *Ut Prosim*. Today the school is a global land-grant university with unique programs and challenges. The school that started with a handful of students now enrolls over 30,000. Harkening back to the school's first commencement address, there are no ordinary moments in Virginia Tech's rich history. The next 150 years promise even more moments that are full of extraordinary possibility and far from ordinary.

A concrete science is a science made up of a knowledge of several sciences. Agriculture is a complex art based upon a concrete science.

The sciences upon which Agriculture is based are Geology & Minerology. To be a successful agriculturalist, it is necessary to understand the laws of chemistry & of animal Physiology, in order to understand how to rear, graze, & market the different animals, and then you must know something of the connection of Agriculture with commerce.

Lecture Aug. 23, 1875.

The first substance in Minerology to which the Agriculturalist should turn his attention is the atmosphere. Pure air is composed of 4/5 N. & 1/5 O. The air is never found pure, but in it is found nearly all the combustible parts of pla[nts].

The combustible part of the plant is from 96 to 98 percent of the plant, all of which is deriv[ed] chiefly from the air. The combustible part of a plant consists of Carbon, Oxygen, Hydrogen, & Nitrogen.

PART ONE

LAND-GRANT MISSION

THE LAND-GRANT MISSION is a central part of Virginia Tech's history. The land-grant concept started in the mid-nineteenth century as a federal program to educate farmers and engineers in the United States. It began in Virginia with the opening of Virginia Agricultural and Mechanical College (today's Virginia Tech) in 1872. By the twentieth century, the land-grant mission had grown to include extension services, home demonstration programs, and other types of outreach for every county in the commonwealth. Today Virginia Tech embraces a global land-grant mission that goes far beyond Blacksburg and Virginia. Despite the changes to the land-grant mission and definition, Virginia Tech has maintained its commitment to providing affordable practical education to qualified students in Virginia and around the world.

A commitment to service, as reflected in the university's motto *Ut Prosim*, is an integral part of the Virginia Tech experience. Service to the community unites students, alumni, and employees. This long-standing tradition to educate others is part of Virginia Tech's historical development. Service is embedded in student life, classroom teaching, events and traditions, and numerous community partnerships and programs. In other words, education is not limited to a classroom on Virginia Tech's campuses in Virginia; instead, Hokies extend it around the globe.

This first section of historical images highlights Virginia Tech's commitment to the land-grant mission and service to the community. There are familiar topics and images, such as student activities, campus buildings, and transformative leaders. This section also includes lesser-known topics and images, such as extension work, experiential learning, community partnerships, and students with diverse backgrounds. Together the images in this section cover the broad historical overview of Virginia Tech's development from 1872 through the present.

The Preston and Olin Building, built in 1855 to house a Methodist school for boys, became the nucleus of the fledgling Virginia Agricultural and Mechanical College (VAMC) campus. Located approximately on the current site of the Moss Arts Center, it contained three recitation rooms, a chapel, and two dozen lodging rooms. Converted for use as the university's machine shops in 1888, the building was destroyed by fire in 1913.

Solitude, the oldest building on campus, served as the home of the Robert Taylor Preston family after its construction in 1851. In 1872 the VAMC's Board of Visitors purchased the home and surrounding 250 acres. The smaller building visible at left housed enslaved families and is today known as the Fraction Family House, in acknowledgment of the contributions made by the Fractions and other enslaved families in the creation and development of Virginia Tech.

Charles L. C. Minor, seated here at far left, served as VAMC's first president from 1872 to 1879. Under Minor's leadership, the new college expanded from a single building to a campus of more than 300 acres. Despite his experience as a Confederate captain, Minor did not believe in strict military discipline for students. This conflicted with the views of Gen. James H. Lane, commandant of the Corps of Cadets. At a faculty meeting in March 1878, the two men got into a fistfight, which led to convictions for disorderly conduct and erosion of confidence in Minor's administration. The Board of Visitors removed him from office in late 1879. Pictured with Minor are VAMC faculty of 1877–1879 (from left): Charles Martin, James H. Lane, M. G. Ellzey, W. R. Boggs, V. E. Shepherd, and Gray Carroll.

In its first year, the fledgling VAMC enrolled 132 students. By the time of this composite portrait (left) of the 1875–1876 session cadet officers, enrollment had nearly doubled, to 255. Among those pictured is the college's first student, William Addison Caldwell at center left (and above detail).

This heavily stylized 1881/1882 view shows what is today the Alumni Mall area, as seen from College Avenue. Pictured at bottom center is the president's house (now a part of Henderson Hall), flanked by a professor's house and the Preston and Olin Building, by that time used as a barracks. At top center are the Second and First Academic Buildings, respectively, with faculty housing on either side. Further to the right are the college workshop (directly above Preston and Olin) and Commencement Hall (with the cupola roof).

V. P. I. Barracks, No. 1 and No. 2.

Cadets assemble in front of Barracks No. 1 and No. 2 in this postcard, likely dating from the World War I era. Completed in 1888, Barracks No. 1 was renamed in the 1950s for James H. Lane, the first commandant of cadets. Today the building houses offices, but it remains the centerpiece of the Upper Quad and retains its central place in cadet life and lore.

Charles Owens began work as a janitor in Barracks No. 1 (now Lane Hall) in 1890 and acquired the responsibility of rousing the cadets 10 minutes before "Reveille" each morning by beating out the tune on his snare drum. One of the university's earliest Black employees, Owens continued to work at VPI until 1909.

In its earliest years, the school's football team had no nickname, being known simply as the "Blacksburg eleven" or "VPI." Later, the team came to be known as the Techs, the Polytechs, or the Techmen. In 1909, the year they won distinction as Champions of the South, the team was first referred to in print as "The Gobblers," a nickname that would remain the official team designation until the 1980s.

Formed in 1893, the cadet band (now known as the Highty-Tighties) is the oldest collegiate band in Virginia. In addition to performing at all home football games, the band frequently appears in local events and national parades. The Highty-Tighties have marched in 11 presidential inauguration parades.

Serving as the university's president from 1891 to 1907, John McClaren McBryde oversaw a rapidly expanding campus and curriculum. Though four presidents preceded him in office, the many changes made during McBryde's term led him to be called the "father of VPI." McBryde and his son developed the university's motto, *Ut Prosim*.

The university was already well into its fourth decade by the time Prof. James Bolton McBryde took this photo in 1906 or 1907. In this section of what was a larger panorama of four photos hand-tinted by Mary Comfort McBryde, the buildings of the Upper Quad are situated in the lower left corner.

Shop classes comprised an integral part of experiential learning during the university's early decades. In this ca. 1892 photo, a small group of students, probably part of a class in forge work, poses with their ball-peen hammers.

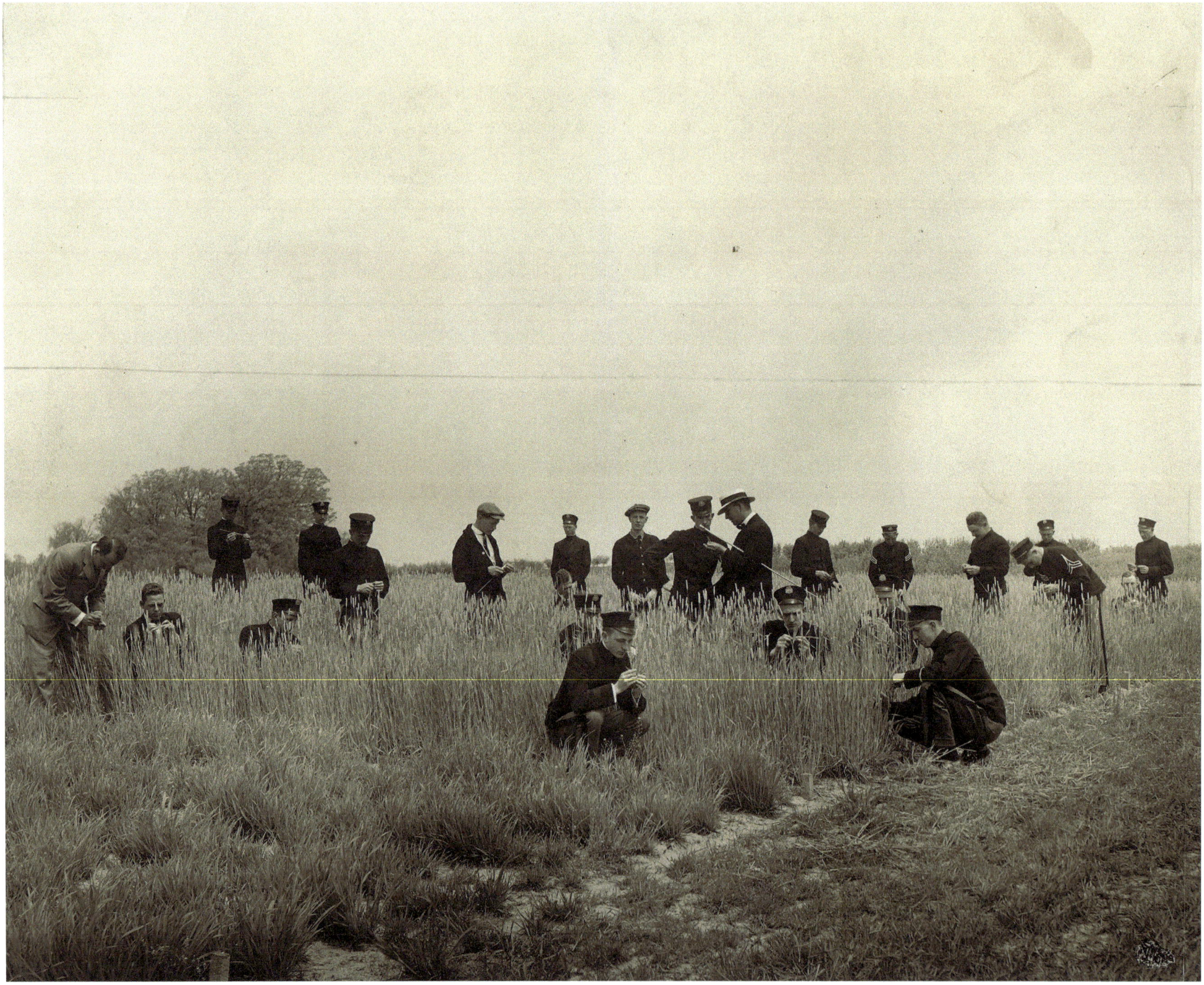

Prior to the improvement of local roads, it took up to three hours to travel from Christiansburg to Blacksburg, so most non-local cadets arrived in Blacksburg via the Huckleberry Railroad, a branch of the Norfolk & Western Railway. This ca. 1910 photo shows the Huckleberry's Blacksburg station.

OPPOSITE: Professor and later president of VPI, John Redd Hutcheson, and students examine the results of an experiment with wheat. Such experiments continue to serve the dual purpose of providing the students with experience and supplying business and industry with useful data.

After a deep snow in 1895 cut off Blacksburg from its coal supply, more than a hundred students volunteered to work with townspeople in clearing a four- to five-mile stretch of road to a mine near Brush Mountain.

The university's Central Steam Plant began operating in 1901 and has been upgraded and expanded over the years. In 1903 it had three 100-horsepower boilers, three steam engines, and two dynamos. In the 1920s, new engines and equipment were installed along with two new motor-generator sets (pictured here). The modern facility includes a 12,470-volt steam-turbine-powered generator, commissioned in 1975 with an output of 6,250 kilowatts. The generator expends steam through an underground network of tunnels that includes more than six miles of steam lines and piping used to heat much of the campus.

After attending VAMC in 1875, T. O. Sandy commenced farming in Nottoway County. In 1907 he was hired as Virginia's first county farm demonstration agent, serving a three-county region. Operating from an office in Burkeville, Sandy and his assistants established girls' canning clubs and boys' corn clubs that became models for future extension work.

Hired in 1910 as the first woman field agent of the U.S. Department of Agriculture, Ella Graham Agnew (left) became a pioneer in home economics education of women, mostly in rural areas. When the Cooperative Extension Service was started in 1914, Agnew was assigned to VPI, where she laid the foundation for 4-H and Extension homemaker clubs. Pictured with Agnew are Mary Moore Davis (center), a demonstration agent who established the home economics degree program at VPI in 1921, and Maude Wallace (right), who served as assistant director for Extension from 1938 to 1959.

Extension home demonstration agents provide instruction in sewing machine repair, ca. 1944. The use of home demonstration agents was critical to Extension's success in improving the living standards of women in rural Virginia. Skilled in the newest methods of home management, these agents were assigned to specific counties (often with an office in the same building as the county farm demonstration agent) where they worked largely with farm women and girls, giving them information and instruction in areas such as canning, gardening, home furnishings, clothing, crafts, meal preparation, health and nutrition, financial and legal matters, and home repair.

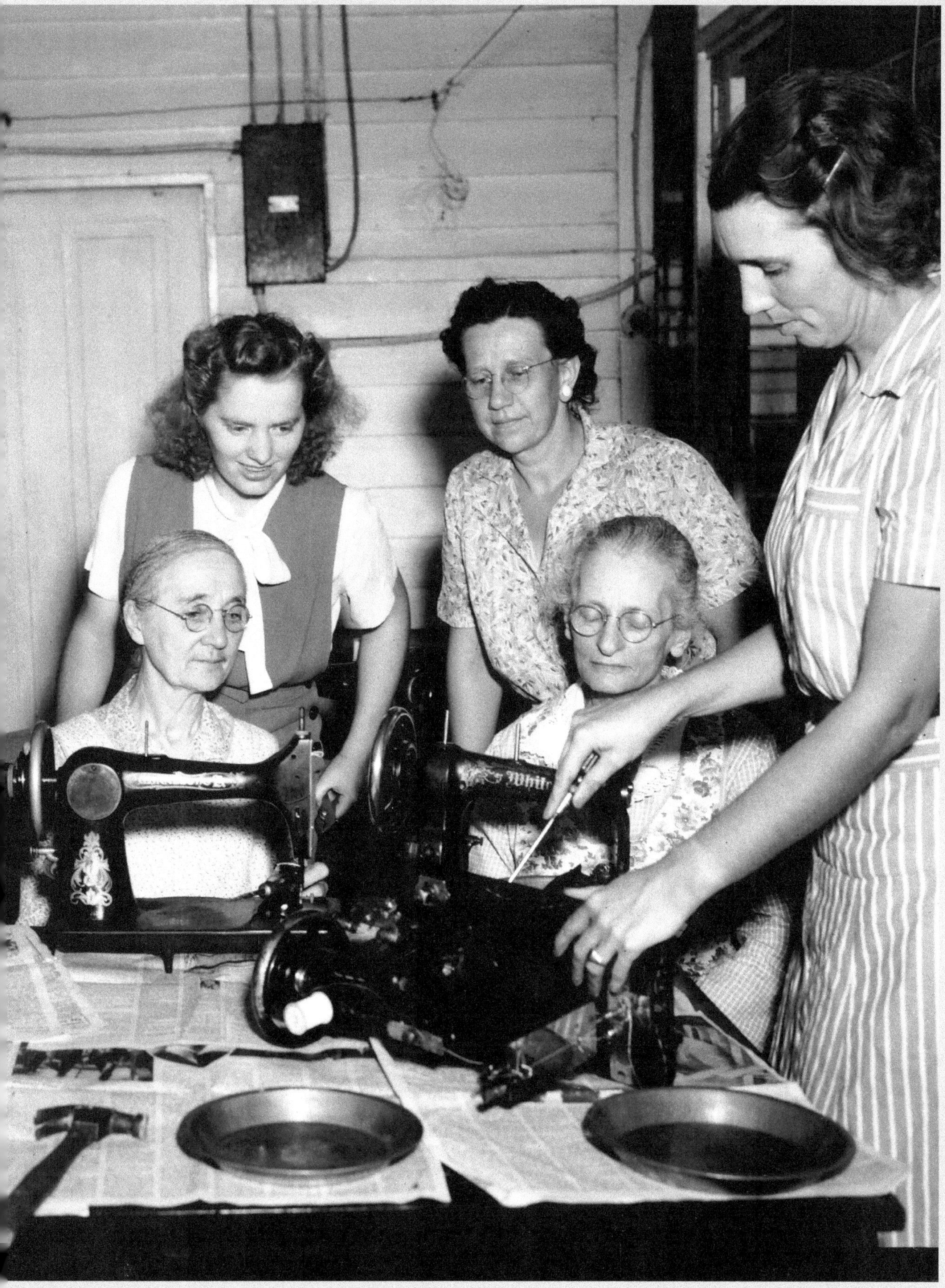

In its early decades, the campus suffered several devastating fires. In this 1905 photo, members of the university community examine the remains of the Science Building following a blaze. Five years earlier, the Rock House, which housed the university's executive offices, was left in ruins by fire. The loss of records in that fire continues to hamper those researching the university's early history.

OPPOSITE: The campus has also experienced an occasional flood. A brief downpour in July 1943 flooded the Lower Quad, pictured here, leading students to swim between their barracks and the mess hall.

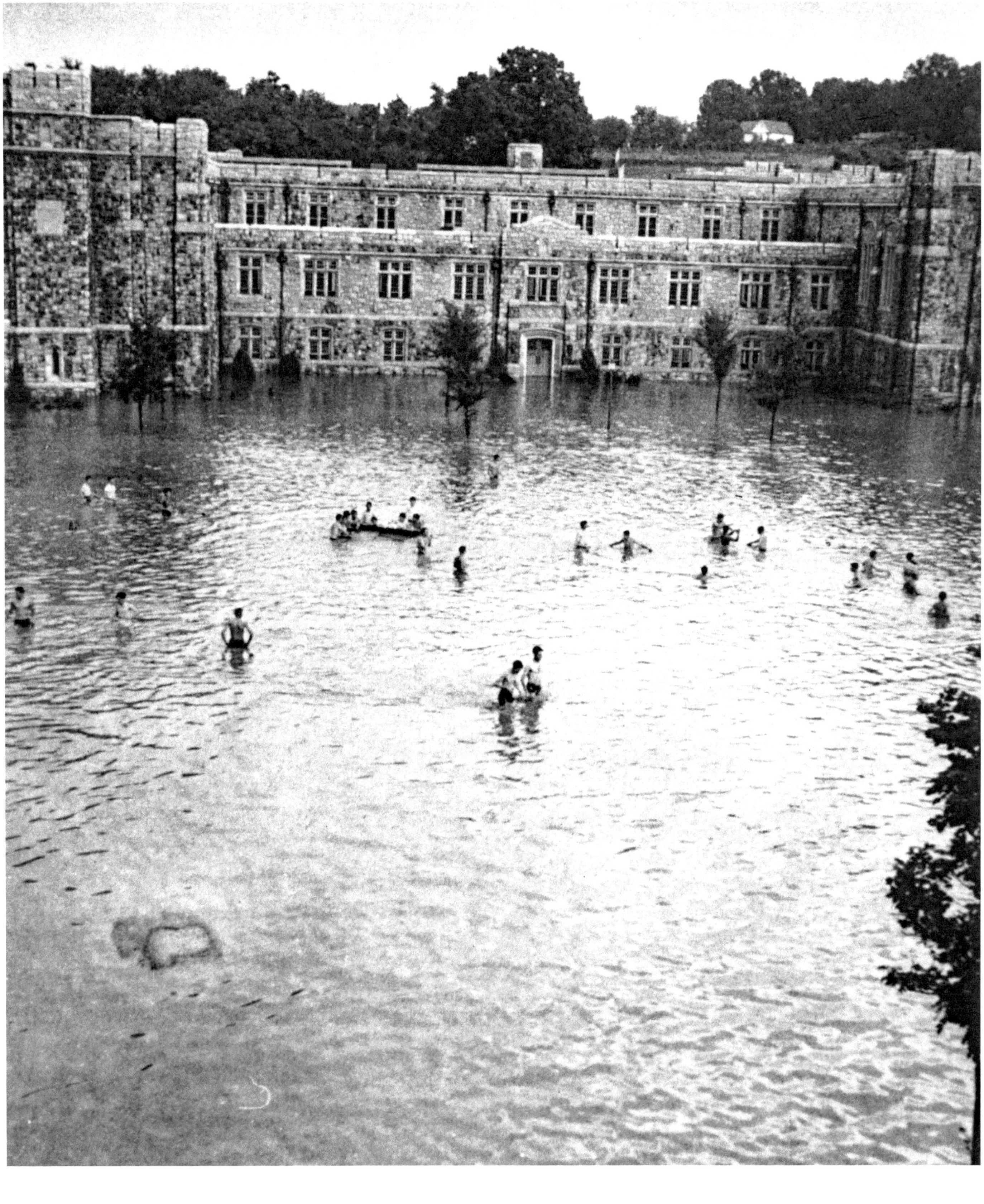

Gardens | Orchard. | Staneer Gardens

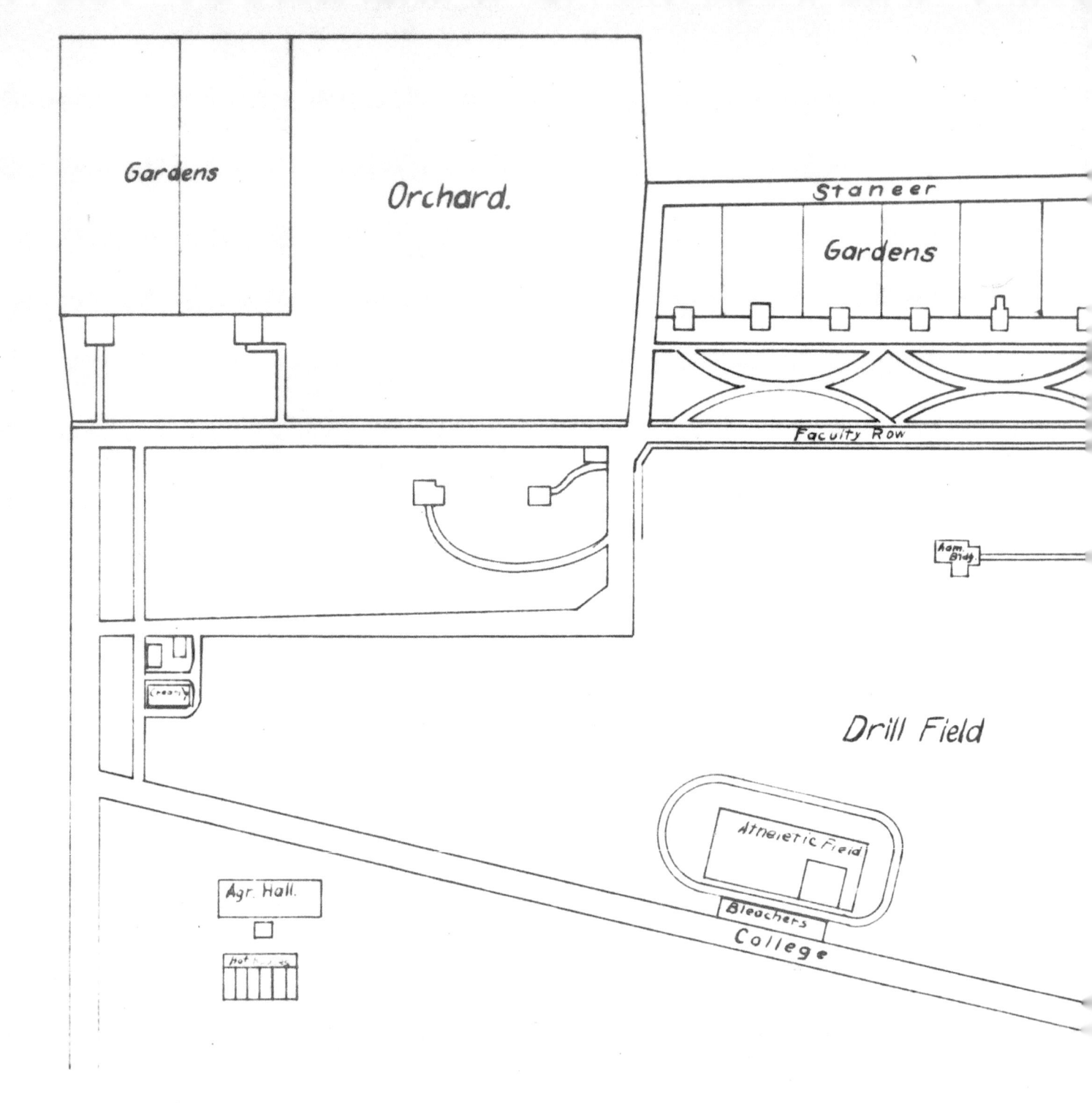

Faculty Row

Adm. Bldg.

Drill Field

Athletic Field
Bleachers
College

Agr. Hall.
Hot houses

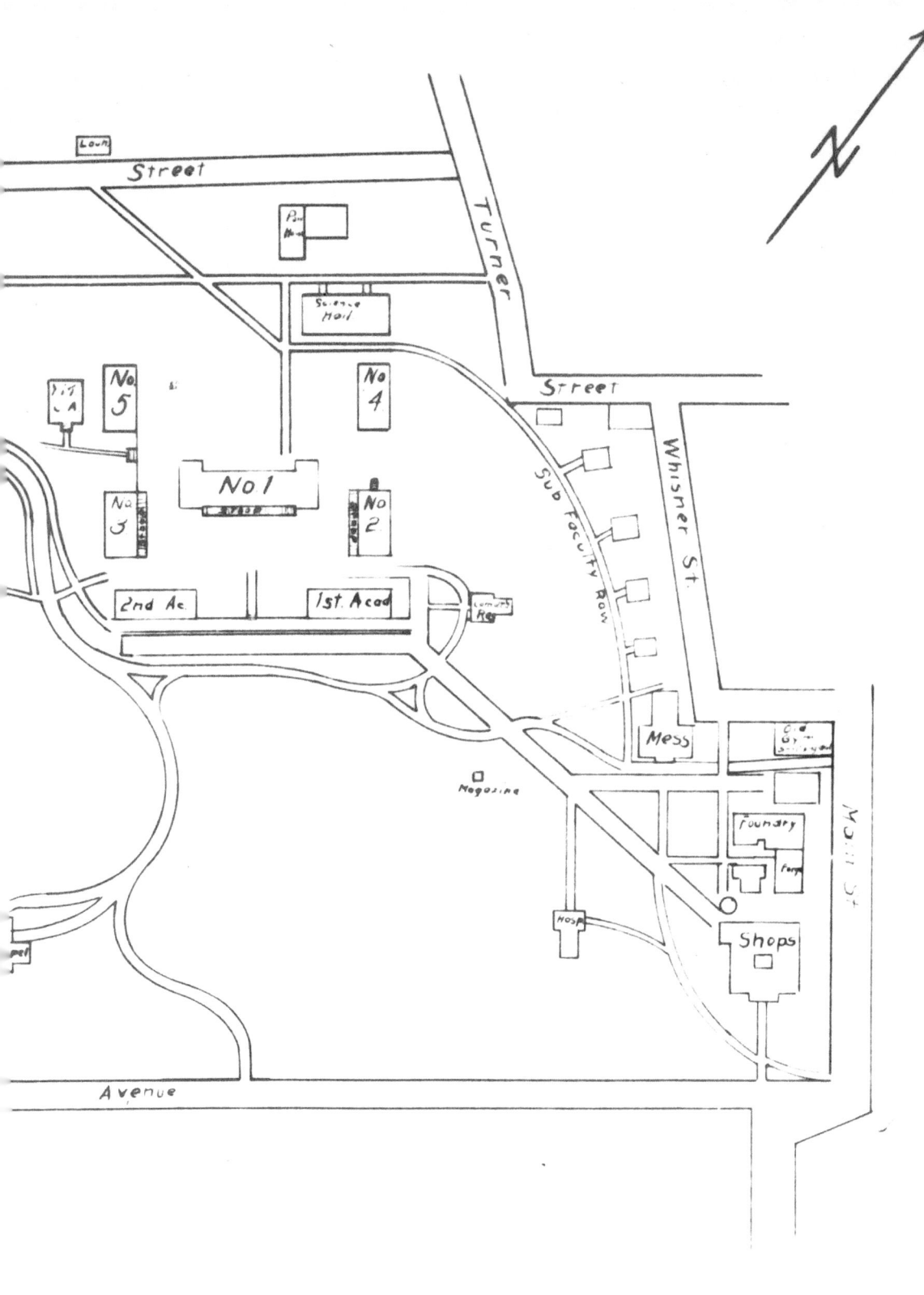

Those familiar with today's main campus, comprising 2,600 acres and more than 200 buildings, may not recognize the less-developed campus core depicted in this 1908 map. As points of orientation, the building in the lower left is Price Hall, one of the few structures shown here that still stands. At the lower right is the intersection of Main Street and College Avenue, with the university's shops located just to the northwest. The building identified here simply as "No. 1" is today more familiarly known as Lane Hall.

In the 1910s the Drillfield was still dominated by simple houses for faculty known as Faculty Row. Students from the class of 1916-1917 are pictured in VPI formation in front of the houses. The administration building is to the right with the top of McBryde Hall (built with Hokie Stone and completed in 1917) behind it.

Crowded classrooms reflected the campus's early growing pains. This photo shows half the students of Col. R. A. Marr's civil engineering course in surveying. A caption accompanying the photo notes that the class of 62 students met in a room measuring 30 × 32 feet, with several students forced to stand.

The tradition of an organized campus snowball fight following the year's first significant snowfall dates to as early as 1896, when the cadets of Barracks No. 1 and No. 2 squared off against one another. In more recent decades, the annual event pits the Corps of Cadets against the campus's civilian population.

Students in a barracks room, ca. 1910. Although the accommodations were undoubtedly spartan a century ago (and were often overcrowded when the university experienced sudden spurts of growth), then as now, residence halls served as a place for gathering, studying, and relaxing.

TECH TRIUMPH

Adopted by Corps of Cadets of
Virginia Polytechnic Institute

VPI

Words and Music by
Miss Mattie W. Epes
and
W. P. Maddux - Ex.-'20

Featured With Success by
Wright's Saxophone Orchestra

Members of the Overseas Club, consisting of VPI students who fought in Europe during World War I, pose in 1920 with The Rock, a monument to 11 students and alumni who lost their lives in the war. Today The Rock is located on the Upper Quad, between Pearson Hall East and Pearson Hall West, and stands as one of several campus memorials to lives lost in war.

OPPOSITE: Adopted by the student body in 1919, the fight song "Tech Triumph" was composed by alumnus Wilfred P. Maddux in collaboration with his hometown neighbor, Mattie Eppes of Blackstone, Virginia. In a nod to the university's military traditions, the rousing number begins with the opening notes of "Reveille."

College workshop showing a lone coed at the center lathe. VPI first admitted women to (non-military) courses in 1921, following a president's report, which noted, "[T]here is some doubt as to whether [women] can legally be denied admission to an institution supported by funds of the state and federal government. The land-grant act makes no distinction as regards sex."

Students in the textile laboratory, ca. 1927. While women enjoyed the educational benefits of their male counterparts, their acceptance into extracurricular activities required more struggle. For example, it would take until the 1940s for the *Bugle* to include women students.

In 1925 Mary Ella Carr Brumfield, Ruth Terrett, Lucy Lee Lancaster, Lousie Jacobs, and Carrie Taylor Sibold (left to right) became the first women to graduate from VPI.

Carmen Venegas was the university's first female international student and first known Latina/Hispanic woman student. Venegas earned one of two scholarships awarded by the government of her home nation, Costa Rica, making it possible for her to attend VPI. She was a member of the American Institute of Electrical Engineers student chapter and a founding member of the VPI Short Wave Club. According to Venegas, when she graduated with a B.S. in 1938 she was also the first Latin American woman to earn an electrical engineering degree in the United States. From *Boston Herald Tribune*, April 21, 1946.

Tek Heung Fung, one of the university's earliest international students, enrolled at VPI in 1920. Fung, from China, poses here during the annual "Rat Parade," then a Corps of Cadets annual rite of initiation, in which sophomores dressed incoming freshmen in outlandish costumes before marching them through town and campus. The practice was discontinued in the 1930s. Fung, here in a top hat and VPI coatee, appears to have been spared some of the worst indignities inflicted by upperclassmen on his fellow "rats."

Initially known as the War Memorial Gymnasium, War Memorial Hall honors Virginia Tech students and alumni who died in World War I. Completed in 1926, the gymnasium hosted the university's varsity basketball games until 1961.

Members of the Virginia Farmers' Institute gather at the Virginia Agricultural Experiment Station farm during a campus visit in 1921. Through performance and sharing of research, the Experiment Station continues to provide the commonwealth and the global community with practical, quality-of-life, and economic benefits.

An early example of the university's ability to share applied knowledge, this exhibit at the Virginia State Fair (ca. 1921) provided farmers with eye-catching, easily accessible information on farm crops and diseases.

In 1925 four VPI agricultural education teachers sat around an oak table to discuss forming an organization for farm boys across the state to develop their confidence and leadership skills through agricultural education. At the meeting were Walter S. Newman, Harry W. Sanders, Henry C. Groseclose, and Edmund Magill, and from their discussions came the Future Farmers of Virginia, which served as a model for the founding of Future Farmers of America in 1928. Here Newman (left) and Sanders pose, ca. 1959, at the oak table (now in Litton-Reaves Hall) where their 1925 meeting was held. On the wall are photos of Groseclose and Magill, and on the table is a mounted plaque that commemorates the FFA's founding. Newman would later become the tenth president of VPI, serving from 1947 to 1962.

Headquartered at Virginia Tech since 1916, Virginia Cooperative Extension (VCE) administers the state's 4-H clubs, located in each of the 108 counties and cities of Virginia. Here, high school students in Suffolk County's 4-H Citizenship Short Course pose with Extension staff in 1964. At back center is likely Hattie P. West, who, after serving as Nansemond County home demonstration agent from 1947 to 1977, was appointed VCE's first Black district program leader of home economics, administering 17 cities and counties.

Blacksburg's small-town atmosphere is visible in Chester Leich's 1930 painting of the South Main Street campus entrance. Seen here is one half of the Alumni Gateway, which marked the transition from town to campus from 1912 until its removal in 1936. In the upper right background is the Military Laboratory Building.

Blacksburg and the surrounding area benefit from university cultural activities and social events not available in other communities of similar size. Lectures, art exhibits, and public performances all contribute to the university's land-grant mission. Campus dances and other social gatherings that were popular in the twentieth century contributed to an active and vibrant local community.

When a fire erupted at the Luster and Black Hardware Company on Blacksburg's South Main Street in 1923, volunteers from the Corps of Cadets rushed to extinguish it. The third conflagration endured by Blacksburg that session, the Luster and Black fire convinced the town to invest in its own firefighting equipment and volunteer company later that year.

Created in 1937 by the damming of Stroubles Creek, the Duck Pond remains a popular campus spot for relaxation and recreation—and for ducks and wildlife. Just above the Duck Pond is the Ice Pond, which served as the college's source for ice from 1881 until installation of the campus's first refrigeration plant in 1898.

Please Do Not
replace books on
shelves. Leave
them on the tables.

A new campus chapel was completed in 1905 on the spot where Newman Library is today. The building also served for a time as a gym and an auditorium before it was converted into the college library in 1915. The above photo shows the exterior of the chapel some years before its conversion to library use. The photo on the opposite page is of the library's reading room around 1932. A fire destroyed the old library in 1953 and Newman Library opened in 1955.

Students dining in Commerce Hall, 1932. While Virginia Tech Dining Services is today nationally recognized for excellence, the plain fare of the early mess halls was not always the best. As one student lamented in the 1900 *Gray Jacket,* "I am so weary of sole-leather steak / Petrified doughnuts and vulcanized cake / Weary of paying for what I don't eat / Chewing up rubber and calling it meat."

The first Ring Dance, symbolizing the transition of students from junior to senior year, occurred in 1934. Announced by a bugler's call, juniors march into the ballroom to a cadence and form the shape of the class numerals. Each couple then receives a pair of ribbons in the class colors to tie their partner's ring on their wrist. As they exchange rings, couples sing "Moonlight and VPI," written specifically for the Ring Dance by composer Fred Waring and lyricist Charles Gaynor. The evening ends with an elaborate fireworks display on the Drillfield and the playing of "Silvertaps." The dance is now held on two evenings to accommodate larger class sizes.

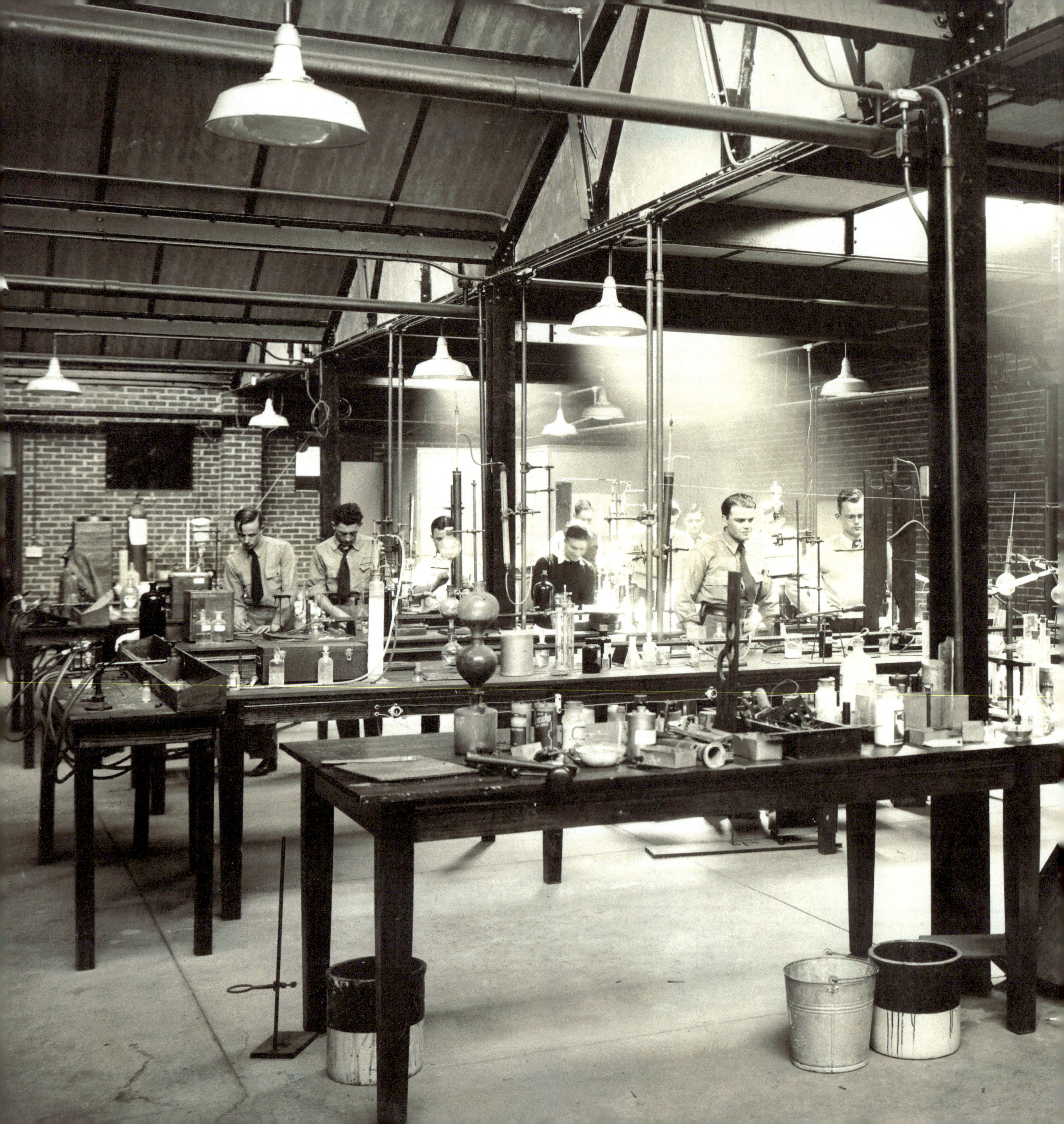

During World War II, military training took on added significance, and VPI became one of more than 200 U.S. colleges and universities to participate in the Army Specialized Training Program, established to help fill the wartime need for skilled junior officers and soldiers. Here, trainees perform calisthenics on the Drillfield in 1943. More than 7,000 VPI students and alumni served during World War II.

OPPOSITE: Practical, or hands-on, learning has been a constant part of the student experience at Virginia Tech. The students pictured here are in a physical chemistry lab in Davidson Hall, ca. 1937.

Following World War II, university enrollment boomed, with returning veterans taking advantage of the G. I. Bill to further their education. Three on-campus trailer courts were needed to accommodate a surge in married students. In this aerial view of the Drillfield's western end, a trailer court can be seen between Davidson Hall and the Duck Pond.

Many students were forced to live off campus with local families or in purpose-built student residences such as Lybrook Row, pictured here. At the corner of Church and Roanoke streets, Lybrook Row served as an unofficial barracks. That it came to be more familiarly known among cadets as "Buzzards' Roost" and "Hell Row" may offer some hint of the living conditions it offered.

In 1954 the owners of Cyrus McCormick Farm (shown ca. 1910) donated the 620-acre Rockbridge County property to Virginia Tech, which soon designated it a branch of the Virginia Agricultural Experiment Station. Today the Shenandoah Valley Agricultural Research and Extension Center offers agricultural producers and extension educators a site for developing new methods of agricultural production while also preserving the farm's historical significance.

In 1953 VPI became the first public university in the South to enroll a Black undergraduate when it admitted Irving L. Peddrew III. An electrical engineering major and member of the Corps of Cadets, Peddrew was prohibited from living on campus and eating in the dining halls, instead staying with the Hoge family, a middle-aged Black couple who lived a mile from campus. Peddrew studied three years at VPI before moving to California to join the workforce.

The first Black student to earn a degree from VPI was Charlie L. Yates, who graduated with honors in 1958 with a bachelor's in mechanical engineering. He was also a member of the Corps of Cadets. In 1979 he returned as a member of the faculty of the College of Engineering before leaving to head the engineering program at Hampton University in 1983. He returned again to Virginia Tech in 1987 as an associate professor in the Aerospace and Ocean Engineering Department before retiring in 2000.

The Virginia Tech Board of Visitors passed a resolution in 2002 renaming New Residence Hall West in honor of Peddrew and Yates. Both men returned to campus in 2003 for the Black Alumni Golden Anniversary Reunion and the building's dedication ceremony. (Peddrew is right and Yates is left.) The first building on campus named for Black alumni, Peddrew-Yates Hall houses the Ujima Living-Learning Community, which is open to students of any background who wish to learn about and support Black culture.

A special Veterans Day ceremony at the War Memorial Pylons in 2017 honored the memory of L. J. Doss, killed while serving in the Army in Vietnam. Doss's name was the first to be added to the pylons since 2012, joining 430 fellow Hokies killed in military action. Construction on the War Memorial Court and 260-seat Chapel beneath it started in 1951 and was completed in 1960. The eight Indiana limestone pylons represent Virginia Tech's core principles: Brotherhood, Honor, Leadership, Sacrifice, Service, Loyalty, Duty, and the university's motto, *Ut Prosim*.

Named Virginia Tech's eleventh president at the age of 35 in 1962, T. Marshall Hahn oversaw a transformation of the school from a mostly male military college into a major research university. Under Hahn, participation in the Corps of Cadets became optional, admissions of women increased, the physical plant expanded, and academic programs broadened. By the time Hahn ended his tenure as president in 1974, the university had added 30 undergraduate degree programs and 20 graduate programs. In this photo taken at Lane Stadium on Governor's Day, October 1974, Hahn (far left) is joined by Virginia Governor Mills E. Godwin Jr. (middle), with the Gobbler mascot looming above them.

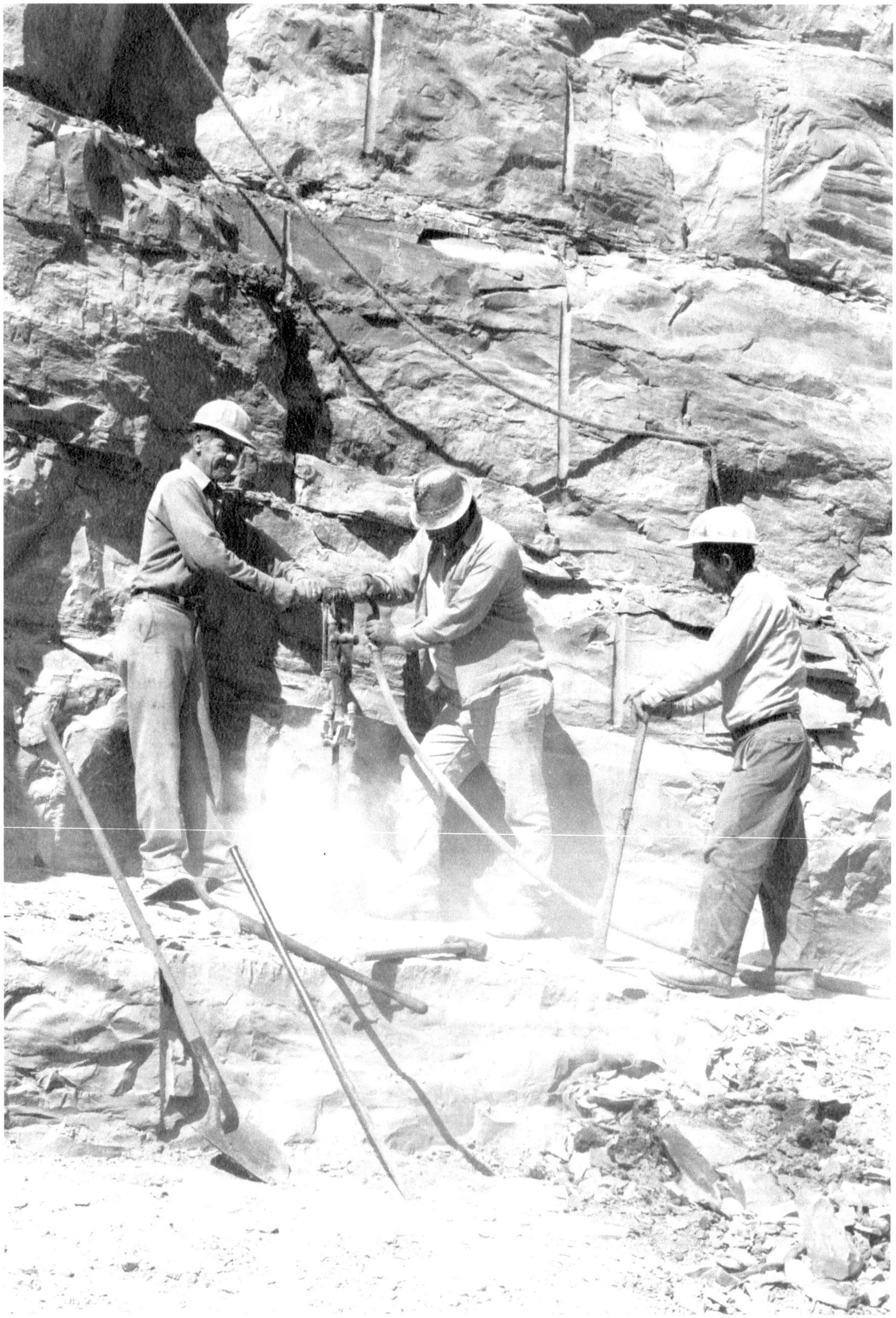

The VPI Airport opened in 1931 on land furnished by the university just south of central campus. Before its construction, air travelers visiting campus landed on the Drillfield. Today the expanded Virginia Tech Montgomery Executive Airport sees more than 16,000 flight operations per year.

OPPOSITE: Workers at the Hokie Stone quarry in 1974. Builders first used the local limestone on campus in constructing the YMCA Building (today's College of Liberal Arts and Human Sciences Building) in 1899. The stone has become a distinctive feature of Virginia Tech's architecture, and a 2010 Board of Visitors resolution mandates that it be the predominant material used in the facade of any new building on the central campus.

Established in 1903 as *The Virginia Tech* and renamed the *Collegiate Times* in 1970, the student newspaper continues to keep Hokies and the wider community informed of campus trends and events.

OPPOSITE: WUVT, Virginia Tech's student-run radio station, began broadcasting on an AM frequency from War Memorial Gynasium in 1948. In 1951 the station moved to Squires Student Center, where it still operates today, serving the campus and local community with an eclectic music mix. WUVT began running 24/7 in 1952 and switched to an FM frequency (90.7) in 1969. Virginia Tech also operates a National Public Radio affiliate, WVTF, through the Virginia Tech Foundation, which acquired the station, then called WVWR, in 1982. Today the station continues to fulfill Virginia Tech's land-grant mission with main service Radio IQ airing news and talk, while companion service WVTF Music broadcasts genres largely overlooked by commercial radio. Roger Duvall, WVTF's general manager since 2018, is pictured.

87

Under Charles Steger, Virginia Tech's fifteenth president (2000-2014), the university experienced its largest growth, with the addition of 40 major buildings, a school of biomedical engineering, and a public-private school of medicine in Roanoke. Steger increased focus on the arts, his efforts culminating in construction of the Moss Arts Center. He also raised Virginia Tech's international profile and helped it become one of the top research institutions in the country. Above, Steger is seated at his desk in Burruss Hall. Opposite, he is joined by First Lady Michelle Obama and Senator Mark Warner at the 2012 commencement.

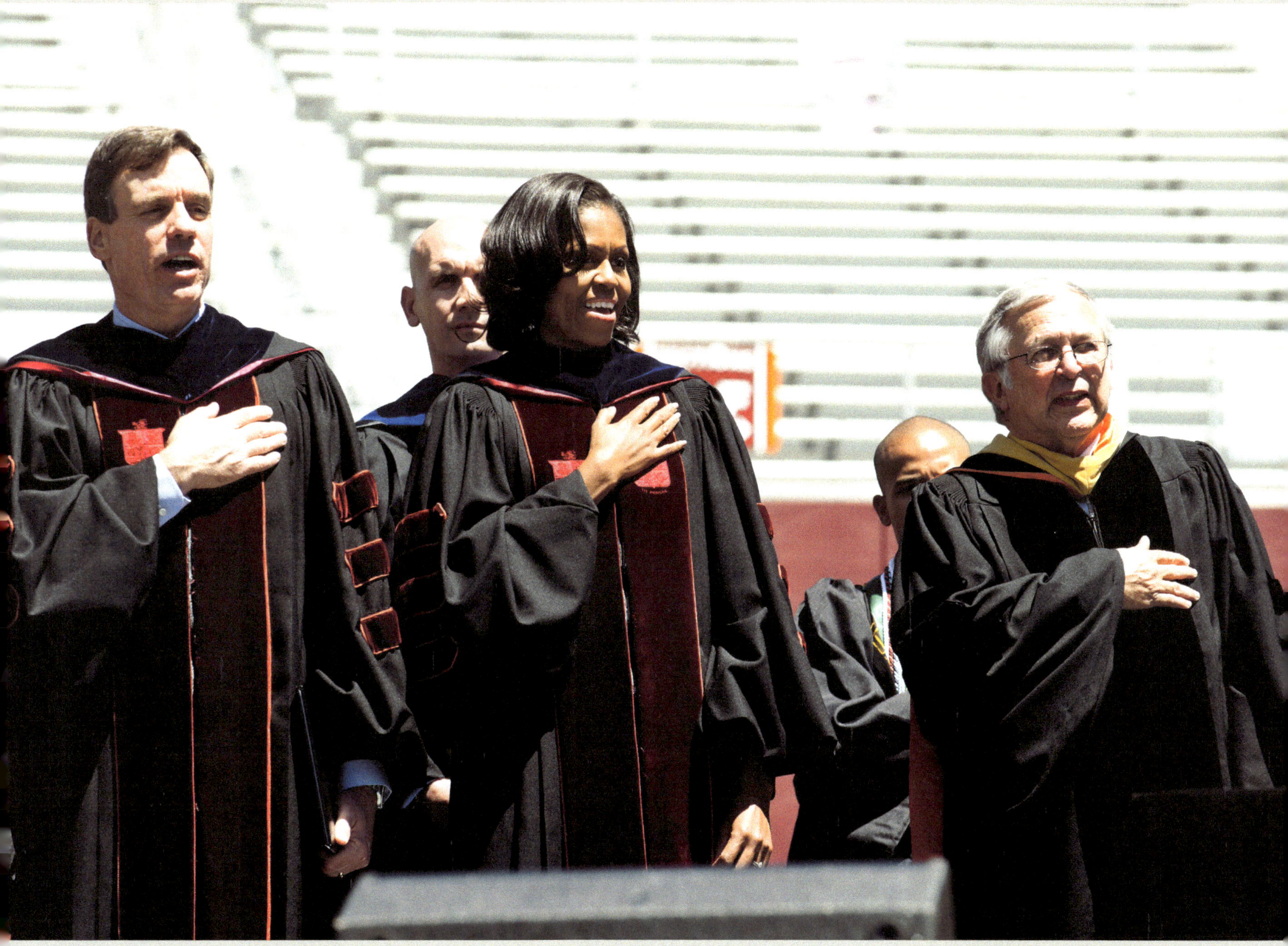

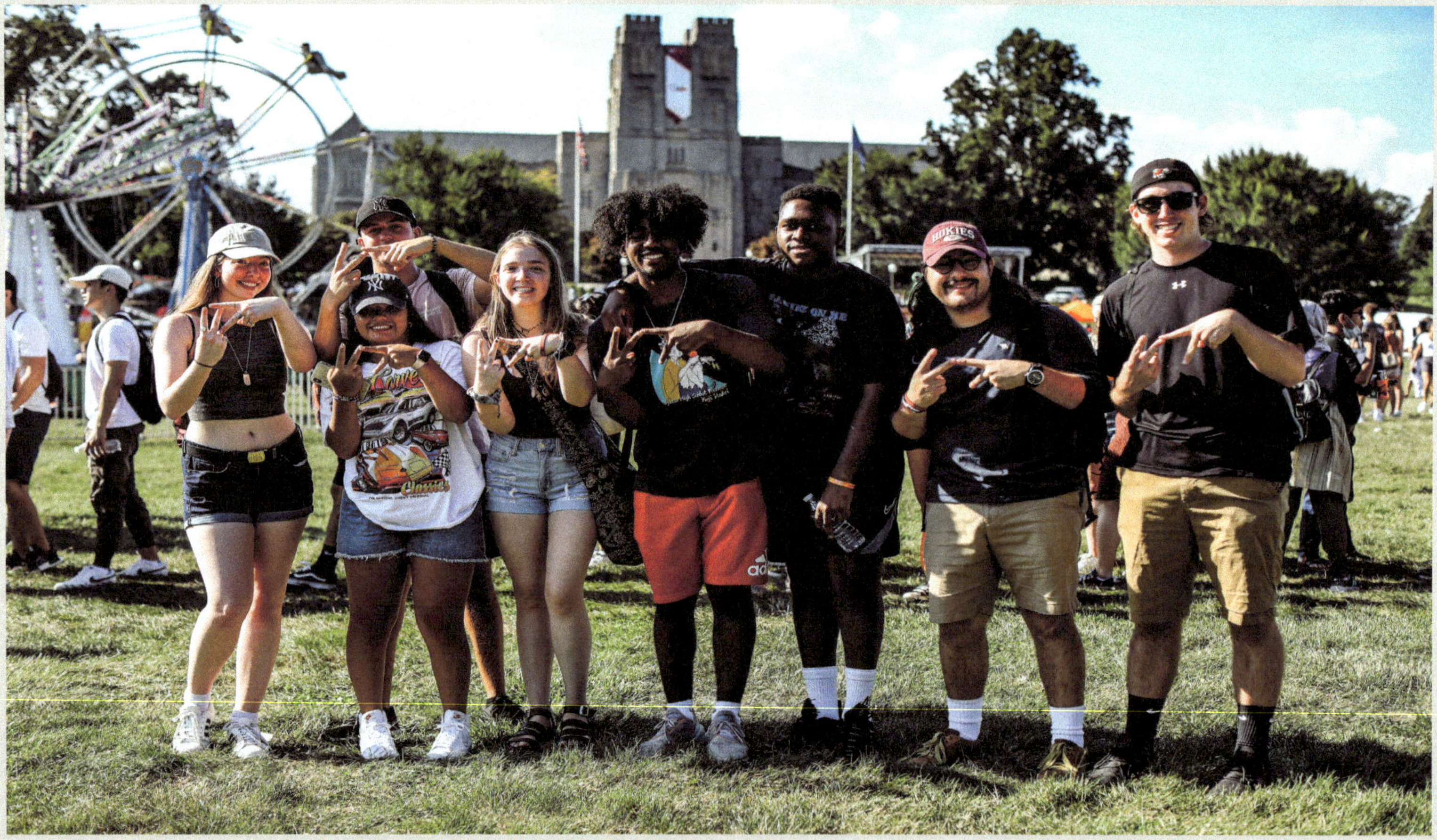

PART TWO

A CHANGING CAMPUS

VIRGINIA TECH has always been an institution that changes and evolves. Throughout its history, new leaders, professors, and students have redefined the school. From the first president, Charles L. C. Minor, through the current president, Timothy D. Sands, each made their imprint on Virginia Tech via reorganization plans, controversial decisions, or anticipating needs that were not always clear or obvious. Similarly, the many generations of students, faculty, employees, and alumni brought significant changes to campus. Virginia Tech's efforts to make campus more diverse, inclusive, and representative of society are still works in progress, but today's student body looks very different from Addison Caldwell's cohort in the nineteenth century.

This section is all about change—changes to the campus and changes to the makeup of the individuals and groups that define Virginia Tech. The images that follow cover the themes of diversity in the student body, athletics, the physical plant, student protests, Principles of Community, the Corps of Cadets and military education, technology, and academic programs. Some of the images will be familiar, others not so much. Taken as a whole, they present a fuller picture of how Virginia Tech's campus and its character have changed over the past 150 years, bringing us to where we are today.

The town of Blacksburg was established in 1798 on 38 acres of land donated by William Black. The original town was a sixteen-block area between the present Draper Road, Jackson Street, Wharton Street, and Clay Street, and slightly northeast of where the Smithfield estate is now located. Blacksburg has grown alongside Virginia Tech, changing with the times and offering small-town charm and amenities to students while benefiting from tourism and technological infrastructure projects thanks to the proximity of a major university. Seen here are two views of the corner of Main Street and Roanoke Street, the first image from June 1922 and the second from September 2021.

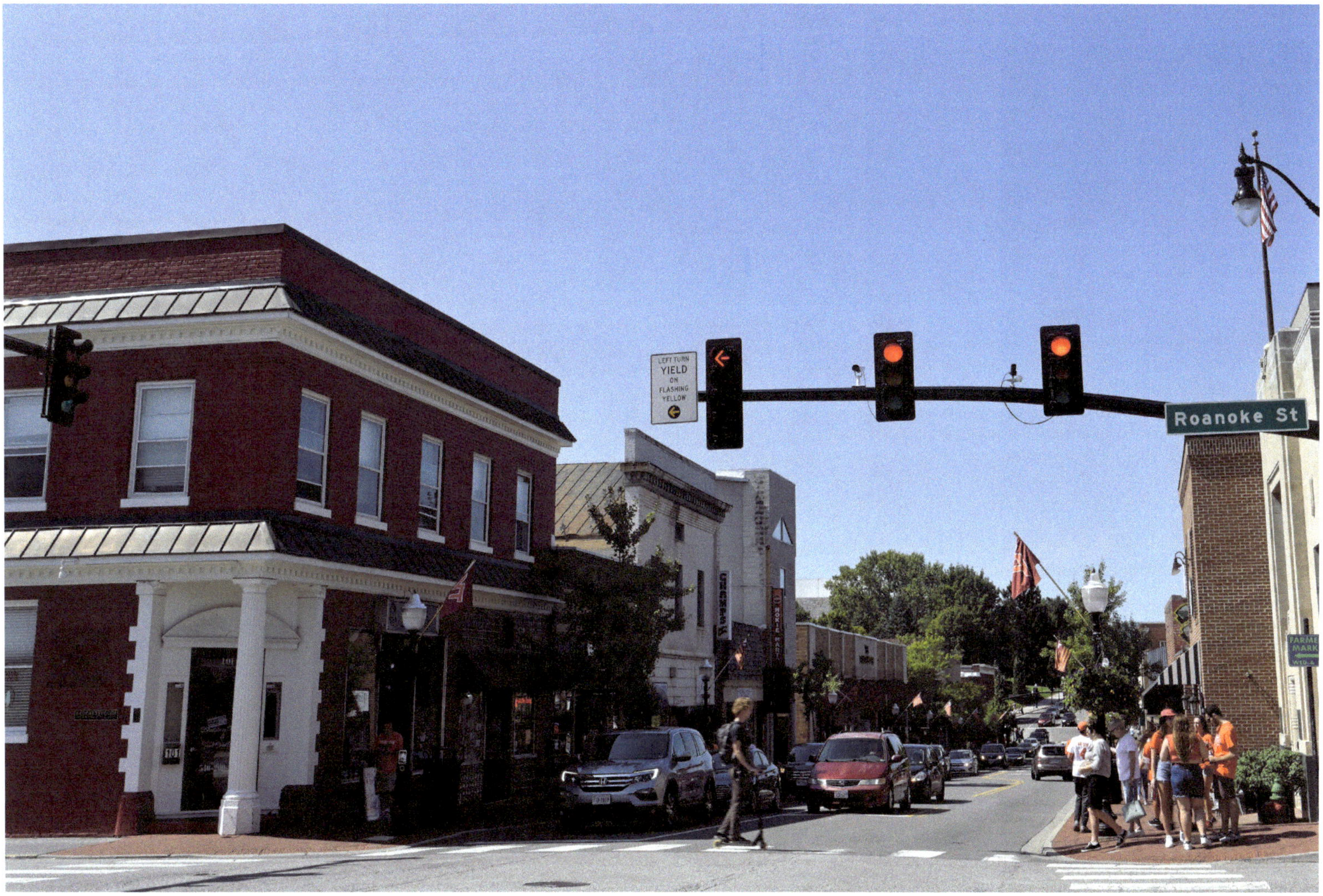
LEFT TURN
YIELD
ON
FLASHING
YELLOW
Roanoke St

Lane Hall, originally known as Barracks No. 1, was completed in 1888 and introduced to campus new amenities including bathrooms with hot and cold running water. In the 1950s the building was renamed for Gen. James H. Lane, first commandant of cadets and professor of military tactics from 1872 to 1881. It was added to the National Register of Historic Places in 2015. Shown here are two photos of the building, the first from the 1890s and the second from a 2017 ceremony when the new Upper Quad flagpole plaza was named for Peter C. Snyder, a 1958 graduate of Virginia Tech who served in Company "G" of the Corps of Cadets.

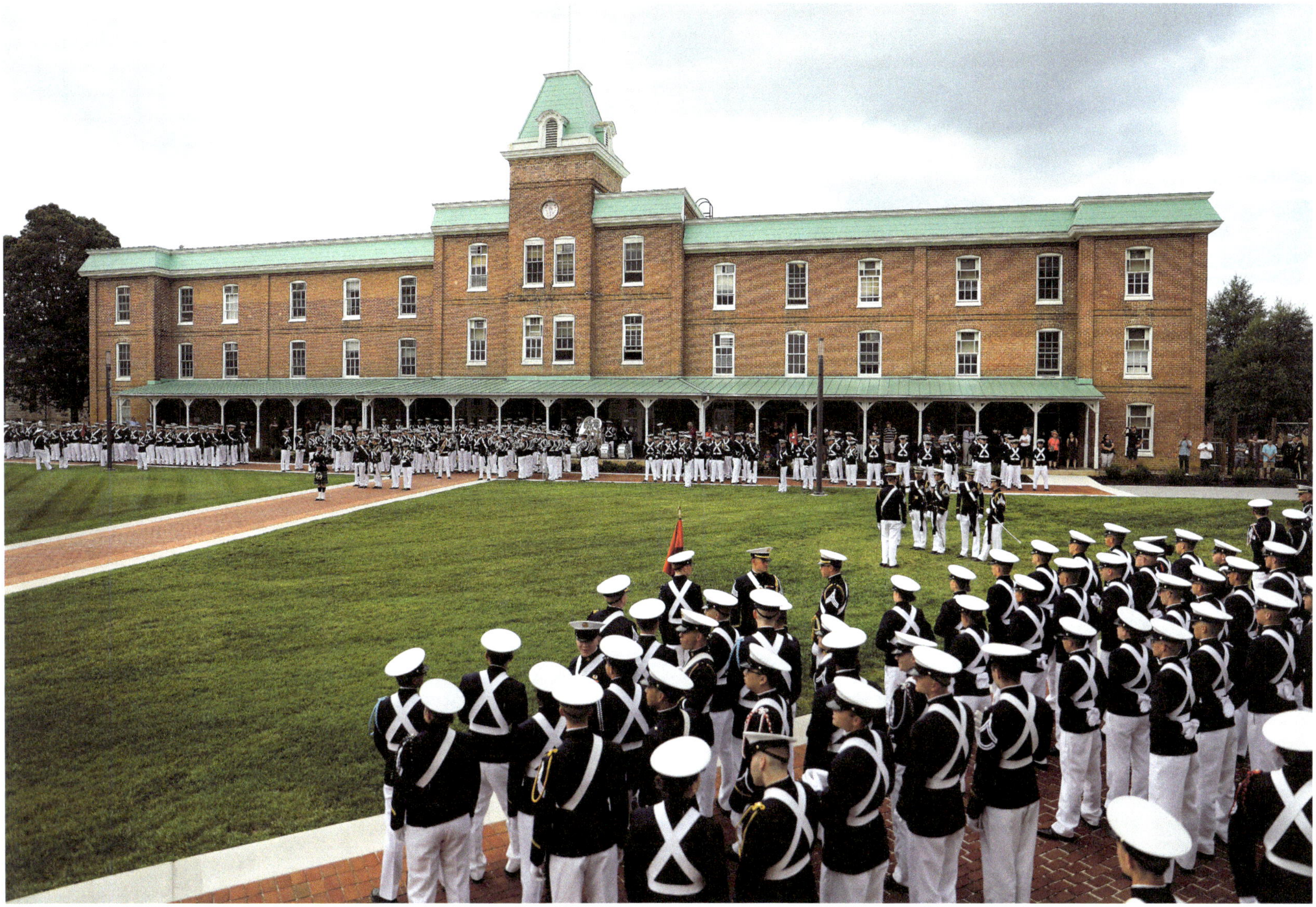

The modern Corps of Cadets is a diverse organization focused on leadership development. At its inception, the Corps was all male and all white, the same as the student body, while the first women enrollees were assigned to a new women-only squadron. When Virginia Tech first admitted Black men, they were added to existing regiments, while the newly admitted women were placed into a new women's squadron called "L" Squadron. Today both women and people of color serve in all squadrons of the Corps. Pictured are members of the Virginia Tech Corps of Cadets crossing the Alumni Mall in Spring 2017.

In 1973 Virginia Tech became one of the first Corps of Cadets in the United States to enroll women, initially placing them in "L" Squadron, a new unit created specifically for women cadets. In 1975 the first woman joined the Band Company, also known as the Highty-Tighties. In 1979 Virginia Tech disbanded L Squadron, and women were integrated into the Corps more broadly.

Opposition to the Vietnam War led to demonstrations on the Blacksburg campus during the late 1960s and early 1970s. The killing of four students by national guardsmen at Kent State University on May 4, 1970, led to the most significant student protest. On May 12, 1970, more than 100 students occupied Williams Hall. President T. Marshall Hahn quickly ended the incident by ordering state police to arrest the protesters, after which he temporarily suspended all of them. Pictured is a student demonstration at the War Memorial Court and Chapel on May 15, 1970, just three days after the occupation.

COMMIES
GET OUT OUT
OF VIETNAM ALSO

DENIM DAY IS WEDNESDAY!

SUPPORT GAY RIGHTS.
WEAR DENIM ON
WEDNESDAY!

THURSDAY,
"WE SPEAK FOR OURSELVES"
A panel discussion on Gay lifestyles
MC BRYDE HALL RM. 113   8:00 PM

GAY AWARENESS WEEK JAN. 15-20, 1979

VPISU GSA GAY STUDENT ALLIANCE

As part of the first Gay Awareness Week in 1979, the Gay Student Alliance (GSA) held Denim Day, asking people in favor of gay rights to wear denim to show their support. While the GSA was effective in getting the word out, going door-to-door and leaving flyers like the one shown on the opposite page, the majority of students did not wear denim that day (even though denim was popular at the time). The event sparked a backlash with thousands of letters of complaint and university administration banning the event the following year. Organizers believed, however, that they had succeeded in raising awareness of gay and lesbian people at Virginia Tech.

The 40th-anniversary commemoration of Denim Day in 2019 drew large support from the university community. Members of the Gay Student Alliance from 1979 are pictured here in the Moss Arts Center posing with President Tim Sands.

In March 2003 students and faculty members staged multiple protests like the one pictured above to voice their displeasure with the Virginia Tech Board of Visitors. The board had recently voted in a closed-door session to rescind the school's anti-discrimination clause regarding the protection of sexual orientation and race, and imposed restrictions on speakers invited to campus. The previous year the board had denied a spousal hire for a vice provost's same-sex partner.

Principles of Community
VT

WE AFFIRM the inherent dignity and value of every person and strive to maintain a climate for work and learning based on mutual respect and understanding.

WE AFFIRM the right of each person to express thoughts and opinions freely. We encourage open expression within a climate of civility, sensitivity, and mutual respect.

WE AFFIRM the value of human diversity because it enriches our lives and the University. We acknowledge and respect our differences while affirming our common humanity.

WE REJECT all forms of prejudice and discrimination, including those based on age, color, disability, gender, gender identity, gender expression, national origin, political affiliation, race, religion, sexual orientation, and veteran status. We take individual and collective responsibility for helping to eliminate bias and discrimination and for increasing our own understanding of these issues through education, training, and interaction of others.

WE PLEDGE our collective commitment to these principles in the spirit of the Virginia Tech motto

UT PROSIM
(THAT I MAY SERVE)

Protests in 2003 led to changes on the Board of Visitors and to the creation of the Virginia Tech Principles of Community, drafted by the Commission on Equal Opportunity and Diversity. The final version, endorsed by the board in 2005, included general statements of the university's philosophy on inclusion and diversity and one against discrimination on the basis of race, religion, and sexual orientation. In 2014 the board approved and reaffirmed the Principles of Community, adding gender identity and gender expression to the antidiscrimination list.

The origins of the Virginia Tech Women's Center began with the creation of the Coordinating Council for Women's Concerns in 1992. Two years later, in 1994, the center opened with three professional staff and five volunteers. Its mission is to promote a community that is safe, equitable, and supportive for women, and that celebrates their experiences, achievements, and diversity.

The Black Cultural Center opened in Squires Student Center in 1991 and operated for decades alongside the Multicultural Center, offering cultural education programming as part of the Department of Student Affairs. In 2016 the Multicultural Center was renamed the Intercultural Engagement Center, and three new centers were opened: the American Indian and Indigenous Community Center, El Centro (the Hispanic and Latinx Cultural and Community Center), and LGBTQA+ Community at Virginia Tech. A year later the Asian Cultural Engagement Center opened. The six centers are now known as Cultural and Community Centers.

DEAR WHITE
people.....

#BLACKLIVESMATTER

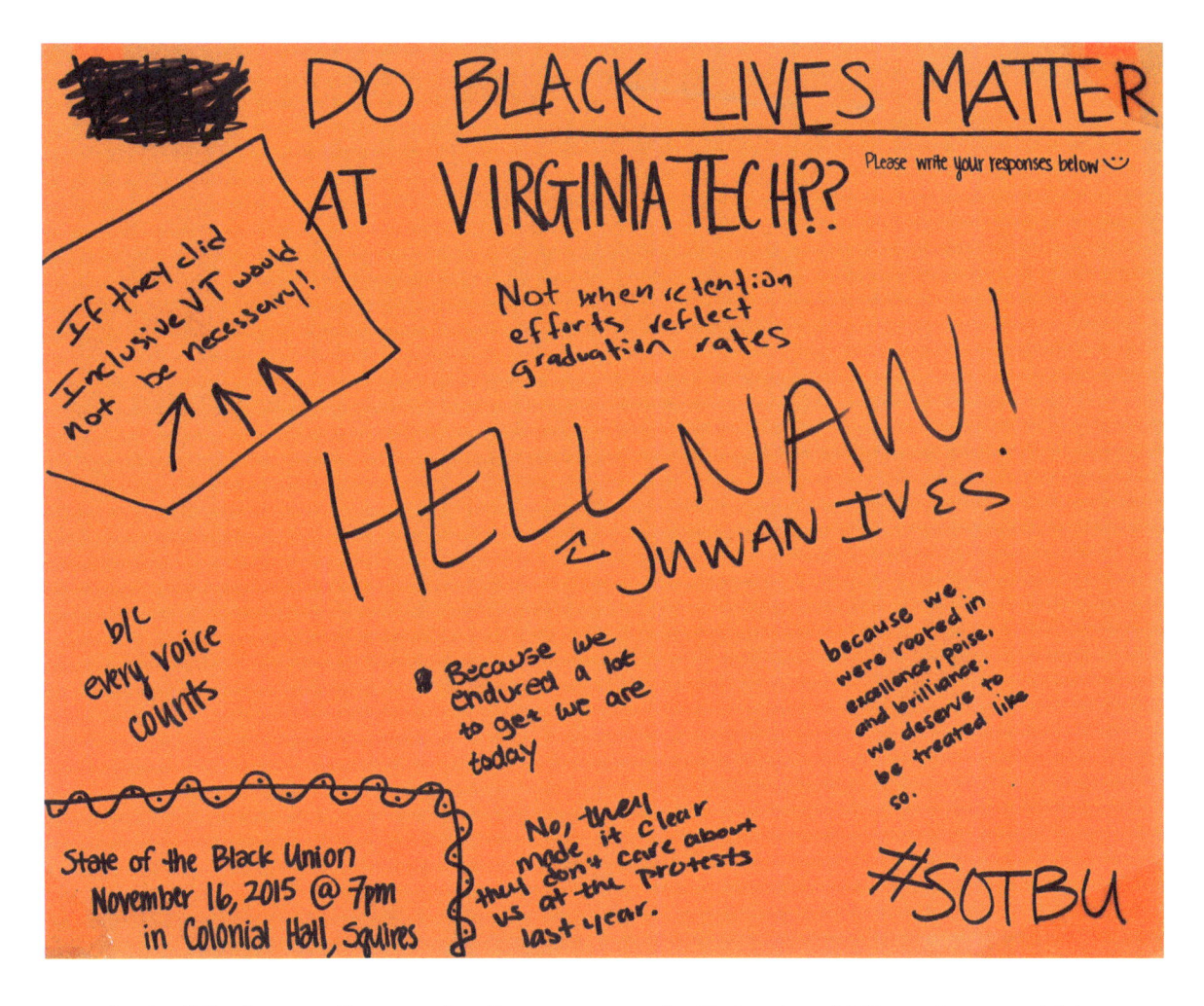

In the fall of 2015, a few months after protests at the University of Missouri over racial inequality, the Black Organizations Council held an event called "State of the Black Union: Do Black Lives Matter at Virginia Tech?" The posters shown here were part of an associated community feedback event that asked students, "Why do Black Lives Matter at Virginia Tech?" Black Lives Matter protests at Virginia Tech mirrored those nationally, and in 2020 they helped reopen discussions about renaming buildings on campus, leading to name changes for two residence halls now known as Hoge Hall and Whitehurst Hall.

Hosted by the Council of International Student Organizations, the Dance of Nations is a night of international dance performances from various countries and cultures, performed by students and community members. This photo is from the 2017 event.

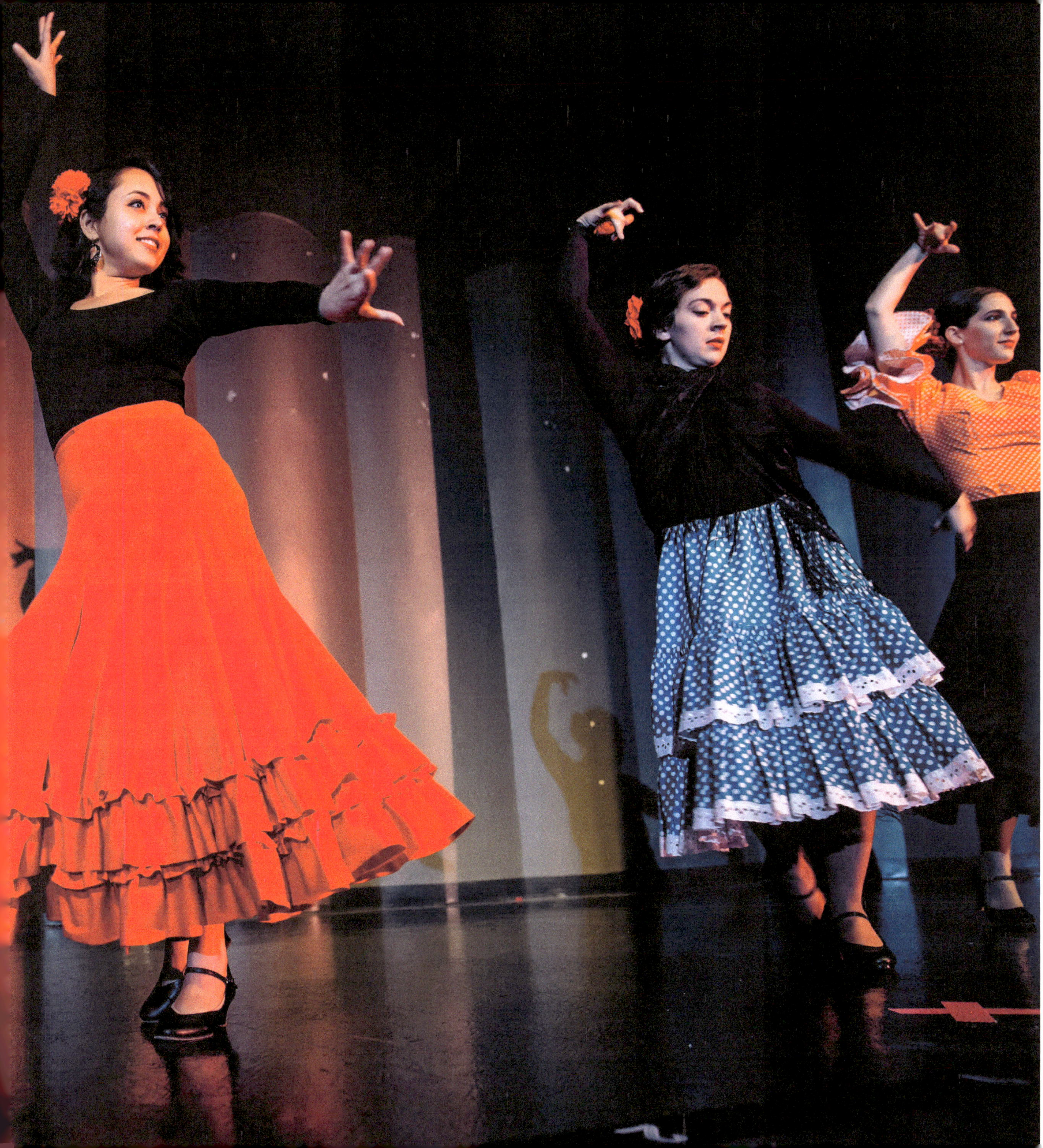

The group Native at Virginia Tech hosted the university's first annual powwow in the spring of 2017. The powwow highlights the diverse cultures of Indigenous peoples in Virginia and has included communities from the entire southeast region of the United States.

A staple of the biennial Virginia Tech Black Alumni Reunion weekend is the Overton R. Johnson Step Show, named in honor of Virginia Tech's first Black faculty member, first Black dean, and first president of the Black Faculty and Staff Caucus. Here alumni and students gather for an alumni-led exhibition step show in Dietrick Hall Plaza in 2018.

TOP: The annual International Street Fair, hosted by the Virginia Tech Council of International Student Organizations and the Cranwell International Center, features food and handicraft vendors, traditional music and dance, kid-friendly activities, and a parade of nations.

BOTTOM: The Indian Students Association sponsors an annual Color War—an event that celebrates Holi, the ancient Indian festival of color and love, while raising funds for charities.

Members of Virginia Tech LGBTQ+ student groups gather at the War Memorial Pylons following the 2019 homecoming parade. The Gay Alliance of Virginia Tech, the school's first LGBTQ+ student group, was founded in 1971. Its successor, the Gay Student Alliance, hosted the school's first Gay Awareness Week, now known as Pride Week. From those beginnings, the LGBTQ+ community has grown, with HokiePRIDE, True Colors, Queer and Trans People of Color, Students Cultivating Change, spAAce, and more student groups all supporting different parts of the broader community.

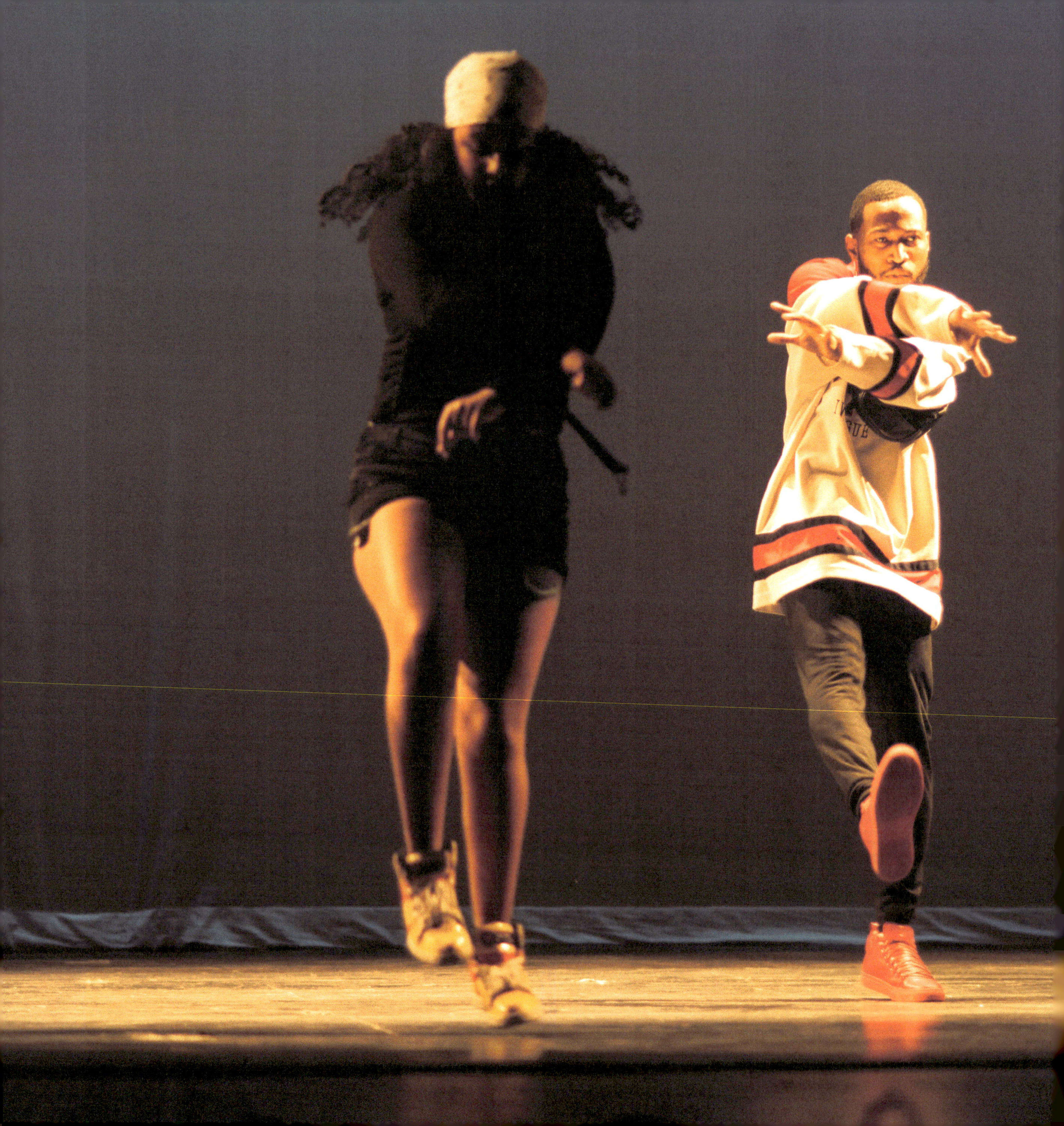

Student dancers perform in Squires Haymarket Theatre before a talk by hip hop artists Kid 'N Play as part of Black History Month 2019. The event was co-sponsored by the Black Cultural Center and Digging in the Crates, a group founded at Virginia Tech in 2016 to foster community and learning around hip hop. Digging in the Crates, along with other groups including the Student Hip-Hop Organization, the Flowmigos, and Students of Hip Hop Legacy, have helped center the hip hop community on campus.

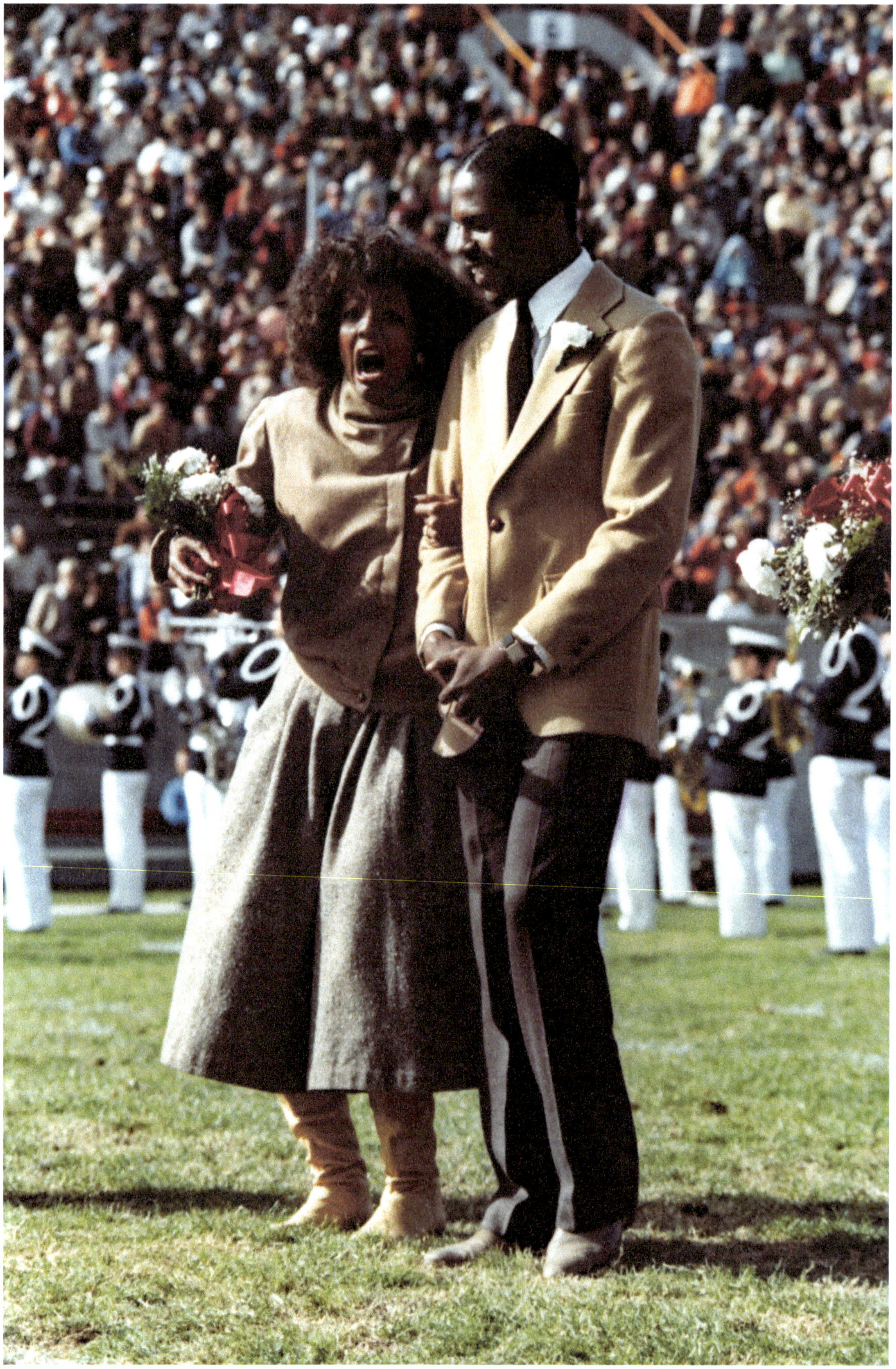

In 1983 Marva Felder, pictured opposite, became the university's first Black homecoming queen. Felder came from a military family in Chester, Virginia; she studied veterinary medicine at Virginia Tech, graduating in 1983 and earning her doctorate in 1987. In 2019, 36 years after Marva Felder's historic crowning, Desiree Velez, pictured above, was named homecoming queen, becoming the first Latina to hold the title. Velez graduated in 2020 with a bachelor's degree in biochemistry.

TOP LEFT: As a teen, Floyd "Hard Times" Meade (1882–1941) took work in the campus mess hall and became an unofficial performing mascot for VPI athletic teams. He first brought a trained turkey to a football game in 1913, starting a tradition that played on the team's name, the Gobblers, and that eventually evolved into the HokieBird mascot.

BOTTOM LEFT: Following Meade, live turkeys continued to be used as mascots under the direction of turkey trainer William Byrd "Joe Chesty" Price, beginning in 1924 and continuing until at least 1953. A costumed Gobbler joined the live turkey for at least one game in 1936, but use of a permanent costumed mascot did not begin until 1962.

RIGHT: Civil engineer Mercer MacPherson led an effort in the 1960s to create a permanent mascot. He worked with a manufacturing company to develop a costume featuring real turkey feathers dyed in the school colors. Known as the Gobbler, it became VPI's mascot from 1962 to 1971, and MacPherson himself originally wore the costume.

TOP LEFT: In 1971 the mascot changed to a long-necked bird standing 7½ feet tall. It was also renamed the Fighting Gobbler at the suggestion of football coach Charlie Coffey.

RIGHT: Ten years later, the Athletic Department was looking to change the Gobbler image and asked the art department for help. Student George Wills designed the new costume that made its first appearance in September 1981 at the Virginia Tech–Wake Forest football game, arriving on the field by helicopter. It was referred to as "the Hokie mascot," "the Hokie," and "the Hokie bird," eventually becoming known as the HokieBird. The costume itself is known as the "diving bell costume" because of the shape of its head.

BOTTOM LEFT: In 1986 there was another push for a redesign, and George Wills, by this time a local cartoonist and illustrator, once again did the design. The new HokieBird debuted in September 1987 at Virginia Tech's football season opener, arriving in a white limousine escorted by the Hi-Techs, and remains the Virginia Tech mascot to this day.

VPI vs UVA

MILES FIELD
BLACKSBURG, VA.
NOV. 8th 1930

OFFICIAL FOOTBALL PROGRAM

Miles Stadium was the home of Virginia Tech football, baseball, and track from 1926 to 1964. Located on Prairie Quad—then a corn field to the south of War Memorial Gymnasium—the stadium was named for Clarence P. "Sally" Miles, class of 1901, who coached both the football and baseball teams and was a professor, dean, and director of athletics. The first football game at Miles was on September 25, 1926, a 47-0 rout of Roanoke College. The following month, the team defeated UVA 6-0 on the day the field was dedicated. The final football game at Miles was a 28-19 victory over North Carolina State on November 7, 1964. The following year the facility was razed.

OPPOSITE: The official football program from the 1930 VPI-UVA game played at Miles Field.

Construction began on Lane Stadium in April 1964 following an effort to raise funds for a facility to replace Miles Stadium. The first varsity football game at the new stadium was a 9-7 victory over William & Mary, played on October 2, 1965. At the time, only the west stands and center section of the east bleachers were open. Most major construction was completed by 1969, at which time the stadium seated 35,050 fans. In 1982 a modern lighting system was added and the first night game was played. Today, after numerous more changes, renovations, and additions, Lane Stadium seats 65,632 and is regarded as one of the toughest places for opponents to play a college football game.

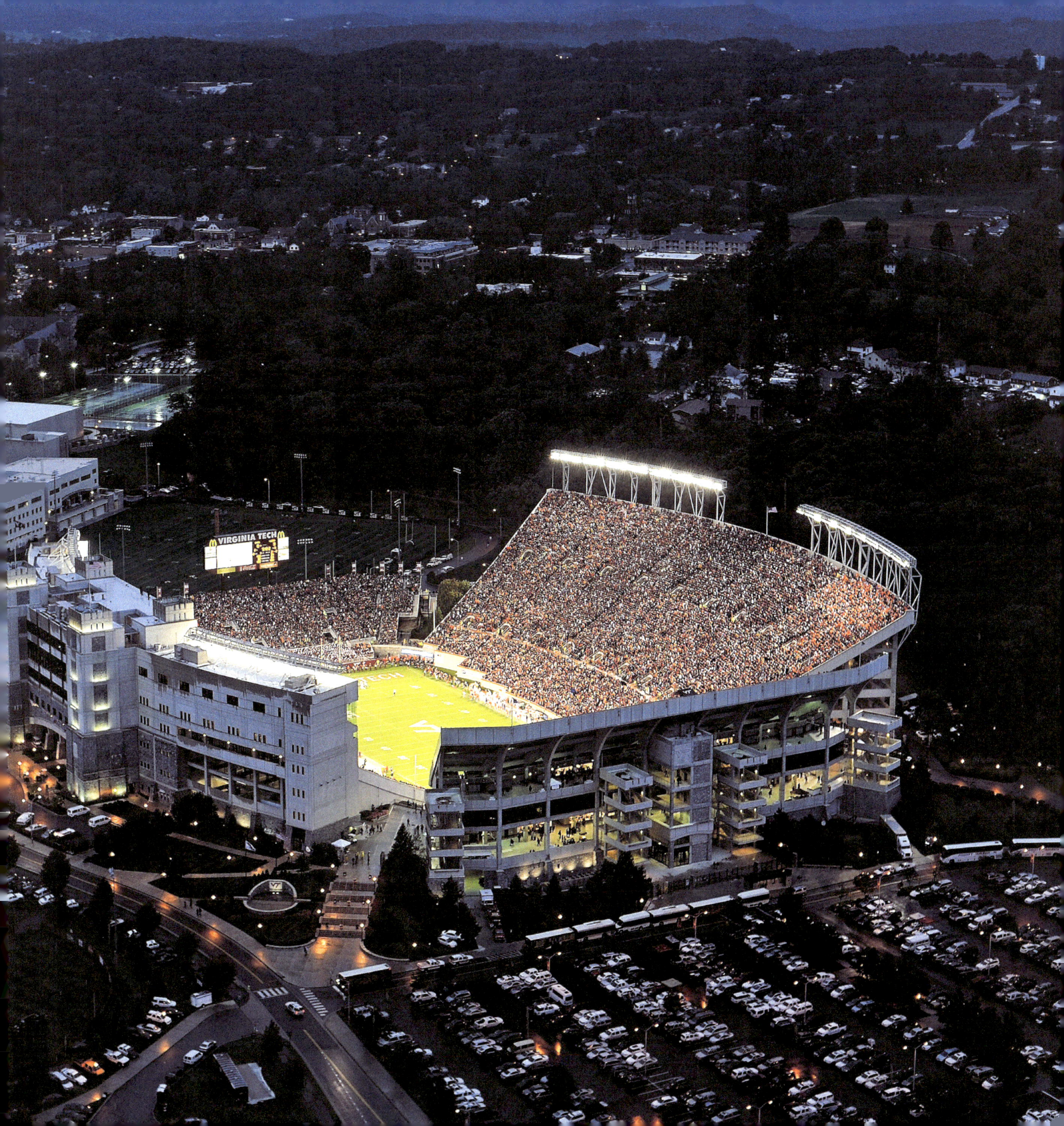
VIRGINIA TECH

Frank Beamer, who played cornerback for the Hokies from 1966 to 1968, served as head football coach from 1987 to 2015. During his coaching tenure, he led the Hokies to 23 straight bowl game appearance (most notably the 2000 Sugar Bowl national championship game), won seven conference championships, and was instrumental in moving Virginia Tech into the Atlantic Coast Conference in 2004. Beamer was inducted into the College Football Hall of Fame in 2018.

OPPOSITE: Vernell Eufaye "Bimbo" Coles scored a total of 2,484 points during his four seasons (1986-1990) on the Virginia Tech men's basketball team, and he remains the Hokies' all-time leader in scoring and assists. While at Tech, he was selected to be part of Team USA Men's Basketball for the 1988 Olympics in Seoul where the team won Bronze, making him the first Virginia Tech athlete to win an Olympic medal. He went on to play in the NBA from 1990 to 2004 and was an assistant coach on the 2006 Miami Heat NBA championship team.

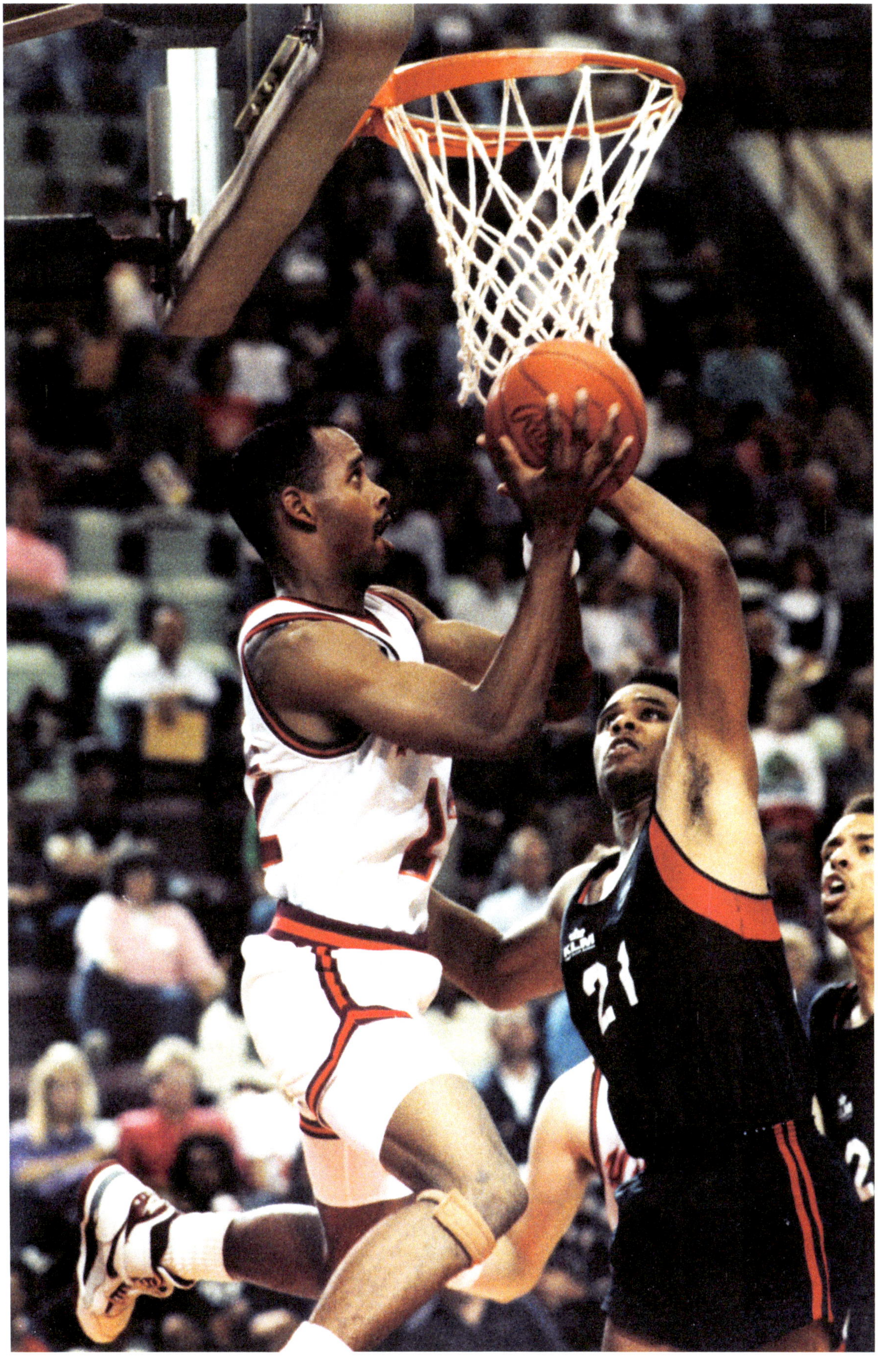
KLM
21

In 1923 Ruth Louise Terrett, one of the first women to enroll at Virginia Tech, organized the first women's basketball team, called the "Sextettes" and later renamed the "Turkey Hens." The 1930 team, pictured here, delivered the first undefeated season with a record of 8-0-1 under Coach (Mr.) Marion Buford Blair. In 1972 women's basketball went from an unsanctioned to official club sport, and in 1976 it became a full varsity sport. In 1994 the women's team played in its first NCAA tournament.

OPPOSITE: Renee Dennis, a standout athlete on the Hokie women's basketball team from 1983 to 1987, set multiple records that still stand today, including Most Points (1,791), Most Field Goals Attempted (1,461), and Most Free Throws Attempted (637). After leaving Virginia Tech, she went on to play professionally in Australia and France before becoming a teacher. In 1997 Dennis became the first Hokie woman to have her jersey retired and the first Black woman inducted into the Virginia Tech Sports Hall of Fame.

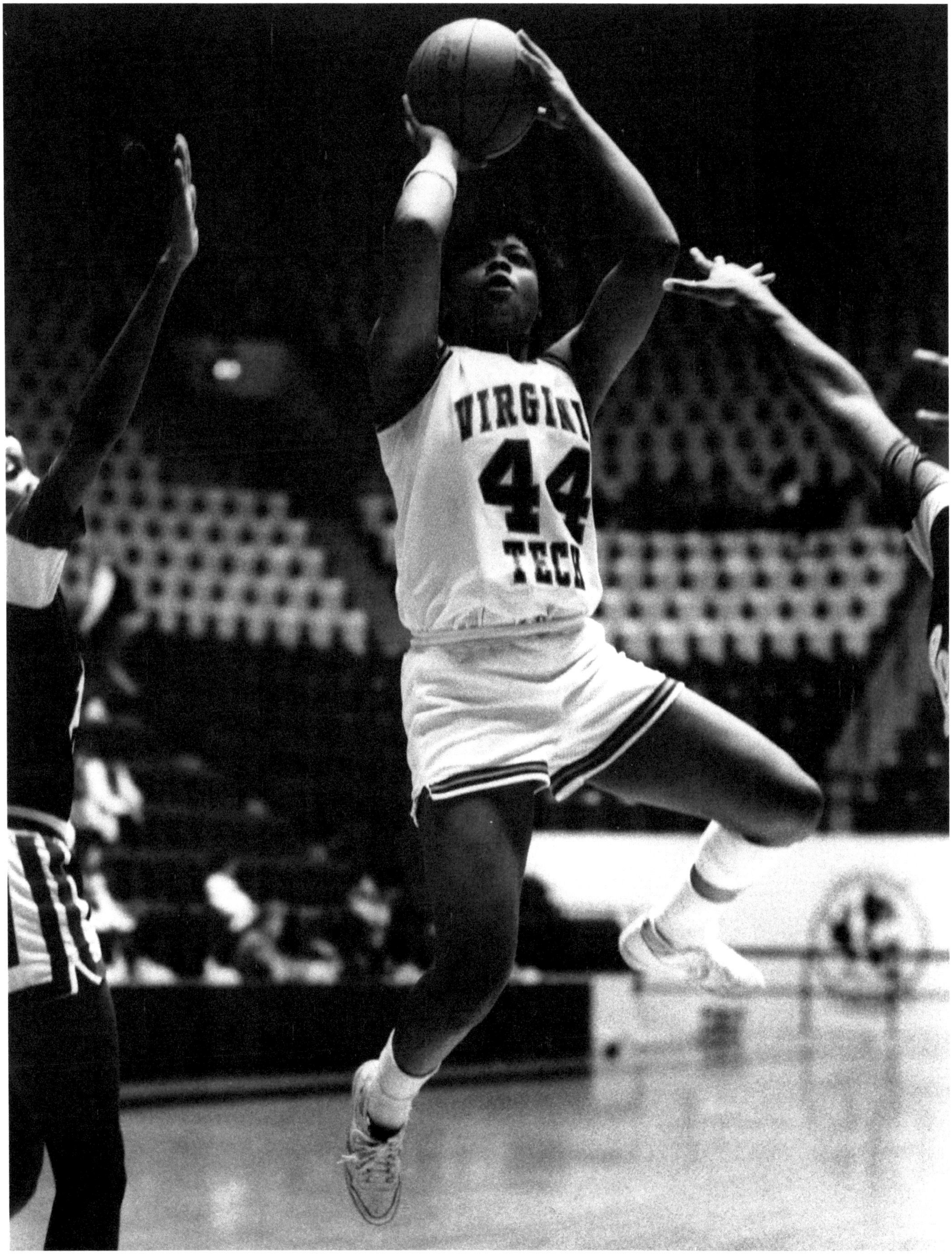
44
TECH

Queen Harrison-Claye made NCAA history in her senior year at Virginia Tech, becoming the first woman to win both the 100-meter and 400-meter hurdles at the 2010 NCAA Outdoor Track & Field Championships. She also won the 60-meter hurdle title at the 2009 NCAA Indoor Championships, making her the only female Hokie to ever win three NCAA titles in her athletic career. A six-time All-American, she competed in the 2008 Olympics in Beijing, reaching the semifinals in the 400-meter hurdles. Harrison-Claye was inducted into the Virginia Tech Sports Hall of Fame in 2021.

Kristi Castlin became the first Hokie woman and the second Hokie ever to win an Olympic medal, taking home the bronze in the 100-meter hurdles in the 2016 Olympics in Rio de Janeiro. During her time at Virginia Tech (2007-2010), she broke multiple school records and was a seven-time All-American and three-time ACC champion. Castlin was inducted into the Virginia Tech Sports Hall of Fame in 2021.

The Virginia Tech Cycling Team is just one of 30 sport club teams supported by the Department of Recreational Sports (a.k.a. "Rec Sports"). Sport club teams represent Virginia Tech and play against other colleges and universities but are not part of the university's NCAA athletics program. The VT Cycling Team competes in the disciplines of road, track, mountain bike, and cyclocross in the Atlantic Collegiate Cycling Conference. This photo is from a 2011 road race in Blacksburg.

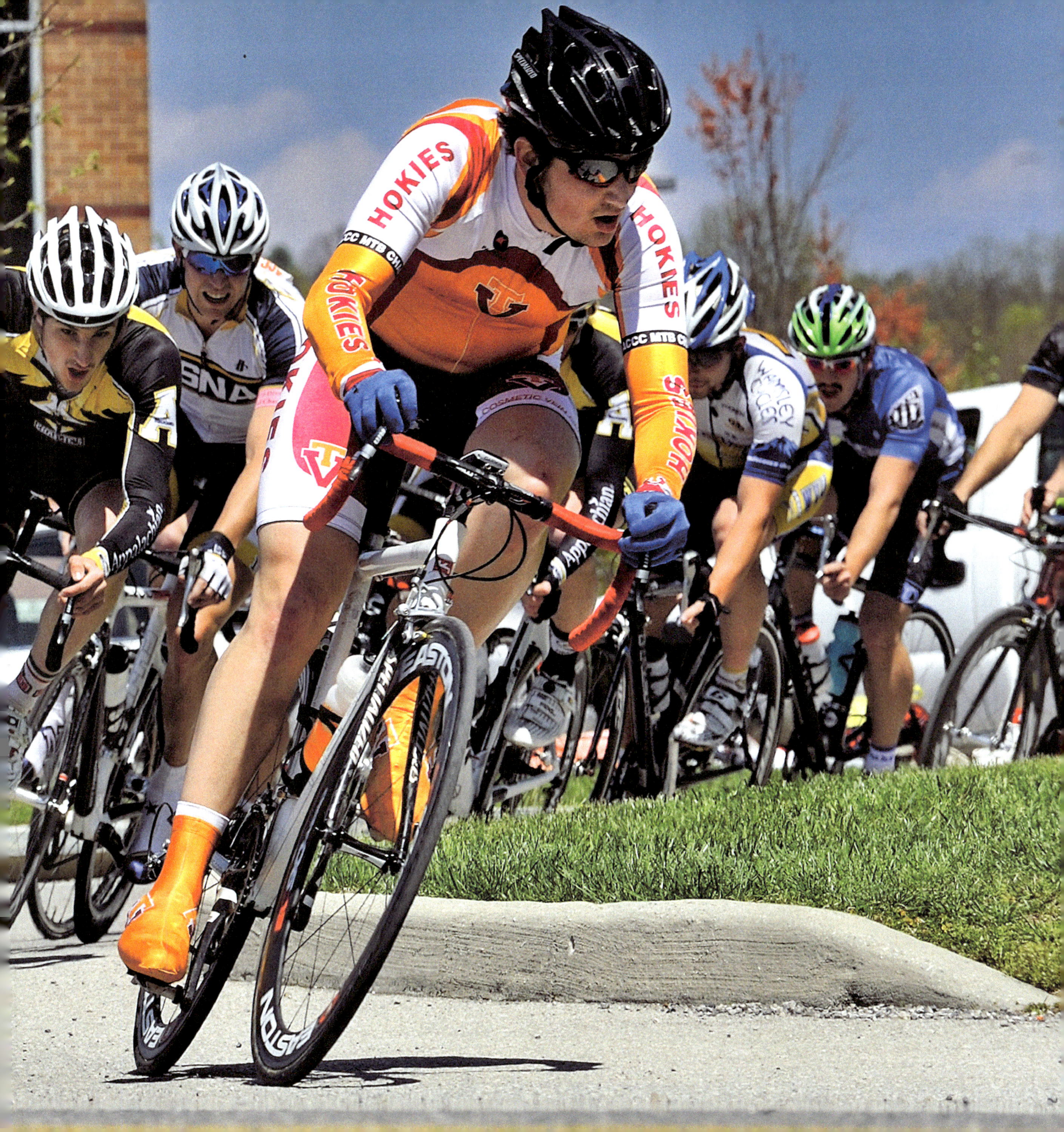
HOKIES
HOKIES
EASTON
Appalachian

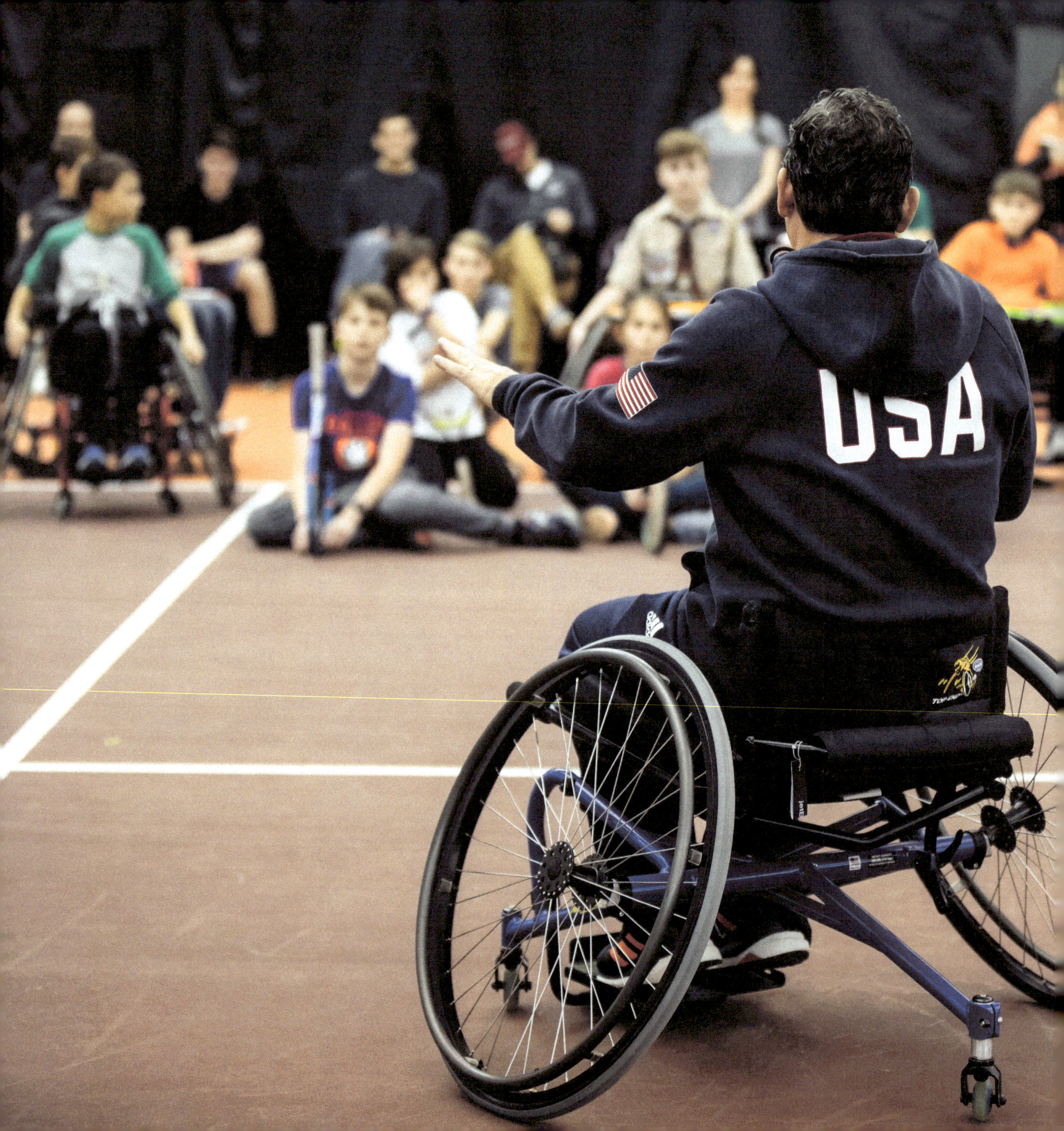
USA

Rec Sports and the men's tennis team partnered, in February 2020, to host a wheelchair tennis clinic, led by U.S. Paralympic coach Jason Harnett, as part of an effort to increase accessible sports in Blacksburg.

On April 16, 2007, 32 professors and students were killed and dozens of others injured by an active shooter at Virginia Tech. To honor those lost, the university holds an annual Day of Remembrance, including a 24-hour vigil at the April 16 Memorial in front of Burruss Hall, the 3.2-Mile Run in Remembrance, and exhibits of condolence items received by the university.

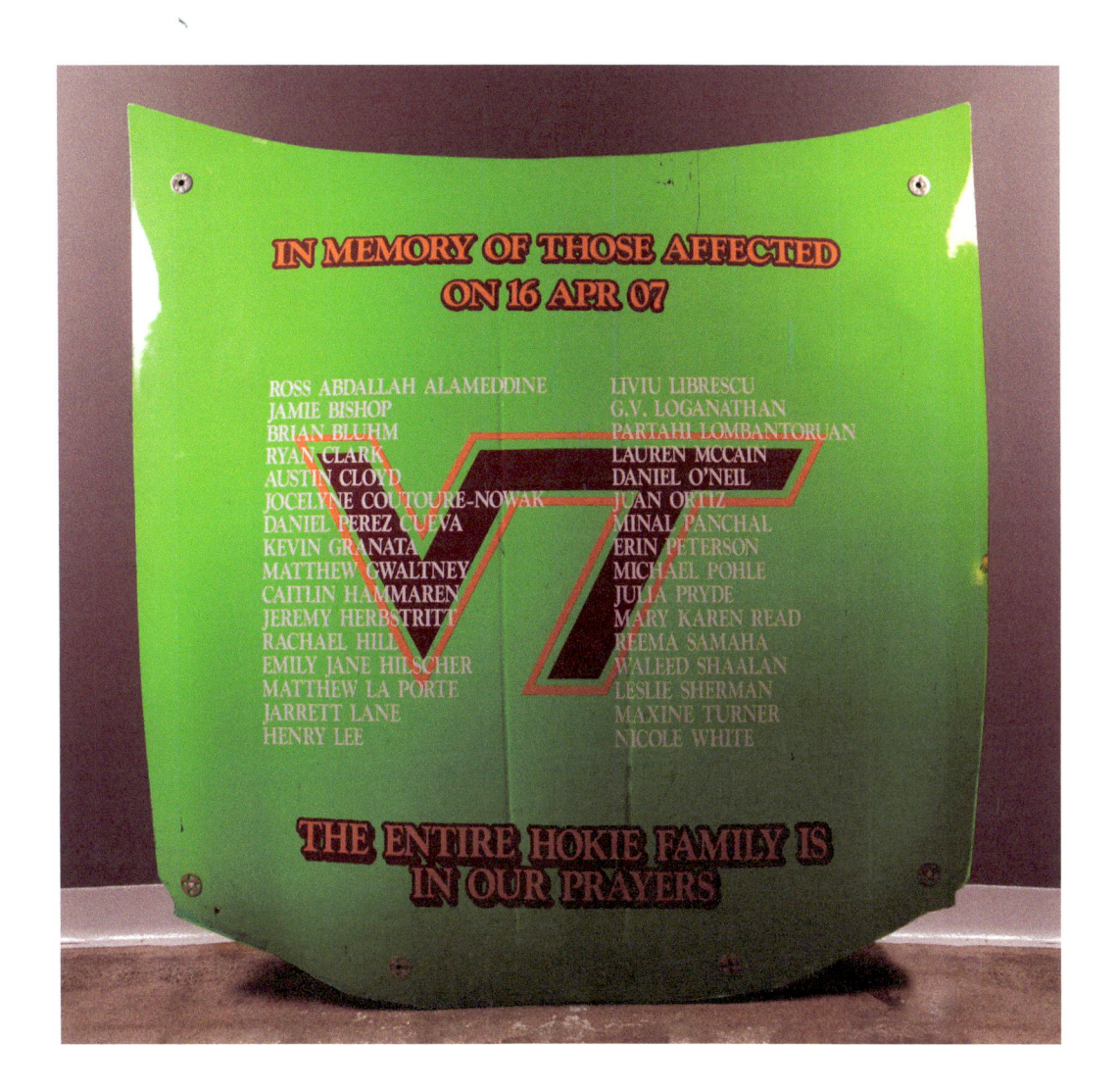

In the days and weeks following the events of April 16, Virginia Tech received thousands of cards and letters of support, posters, banners, art, poetry, wreaths, memory books, and other unique items from around the world. One such item is this lime-green hood from a racecar driven by Dave Butler at Langley Speedway. It bears the names of those killed on April 16. Special Collections and University Archives were given responsibility for inventorying, photographing, and preserving these condolence items in the Virginia Tech April 16, 2007 Archives of the University Libraries.

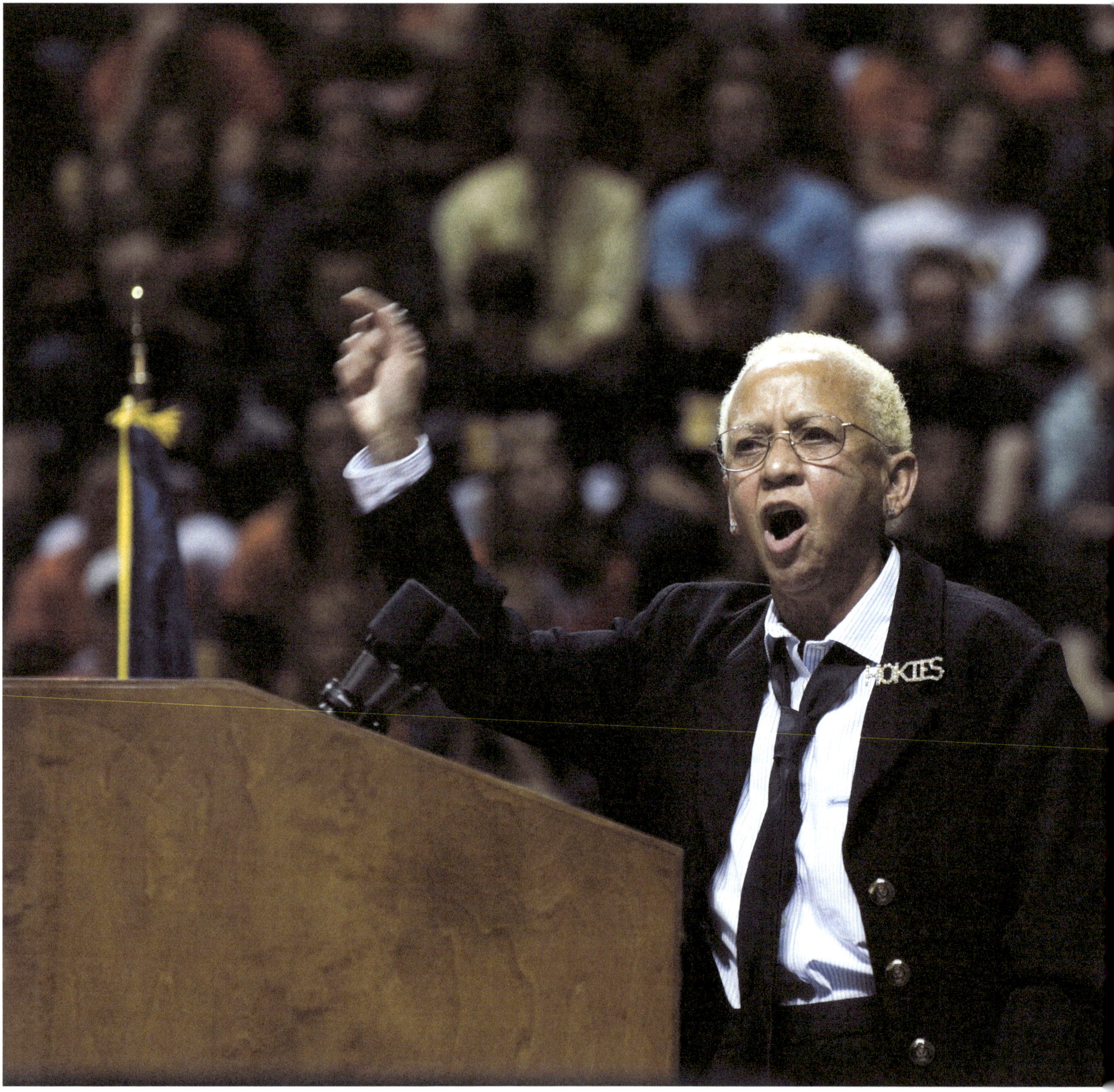

A convocation in Cassell Coliseum on April 17 provided the first opportunity for the Virginia Tech community to gather and share its collective grief following the tragedy. Among the speakers were President George W. Bush, Virginia Governor Tim Kaine, Virginia Tech President Charles Steger, and Virginia Tech Professor Nikki Giovanni. After Giovanni finished reading her stirring poem, "We Are Virginia Tech," the capacity crowd rose to its feet cheering and chanted, "Let's Go, Hokies."

Virginia Cooperative Extension leverages a network of faculty at two universities (Virginia Tech and Virginia State University), 108 county and city offices, 11 Agricultural Research and Extension Centers (ARECs), and six 4-H educational centers. Pictured here is Robin White of the Department of Animal and Poultry Sciences, examining a horse at the Middleburg Agricultural Research and Extension (MARE) Center in 2019.

The Alson H. Smith Jr. AREC in Winchester serves Virginia's commercial tree fruit and wine-grape industries through extensive research and programming. Pictured here is Mizuho Nita, an Extension specialist and faculty member in the Department of Plant Pathology, showing an infected grape vine at the Winchester facility. Nita's research focuses on the development of biologically, environmentally, and economically sound disease management tools.

The Virginia-Maryland College of Veterinary Medicine (VMCVM) broke ground in 1979, during the presidency of William E. Lavery, Virginia Tech's twelfth president (left in photo). In addition to the main campus in Blacksburg, the college operates the Animal Cancer Care and Research Center in Roanoke, the Marion duPont Scott Equine Medical Center in Leesburg, and the Avrum Gudelsky Veterinary Medicine Center in College Park, Maryland.

TOP: Lauren Dodd, a two-time graduate of VMCVM, was a resident in clinical nutrition in 2019 when her master of public health capstone project—popularly known as the "Fat Cat Study"—was picked up by media outlets nationwide.

BOTTOM: Saint, a retired Saint Francis service dog from Roanoke, made one of his regular visits to VMCVM in 2020 for rehabilitative services to improve his mobility and hind leg weakness.

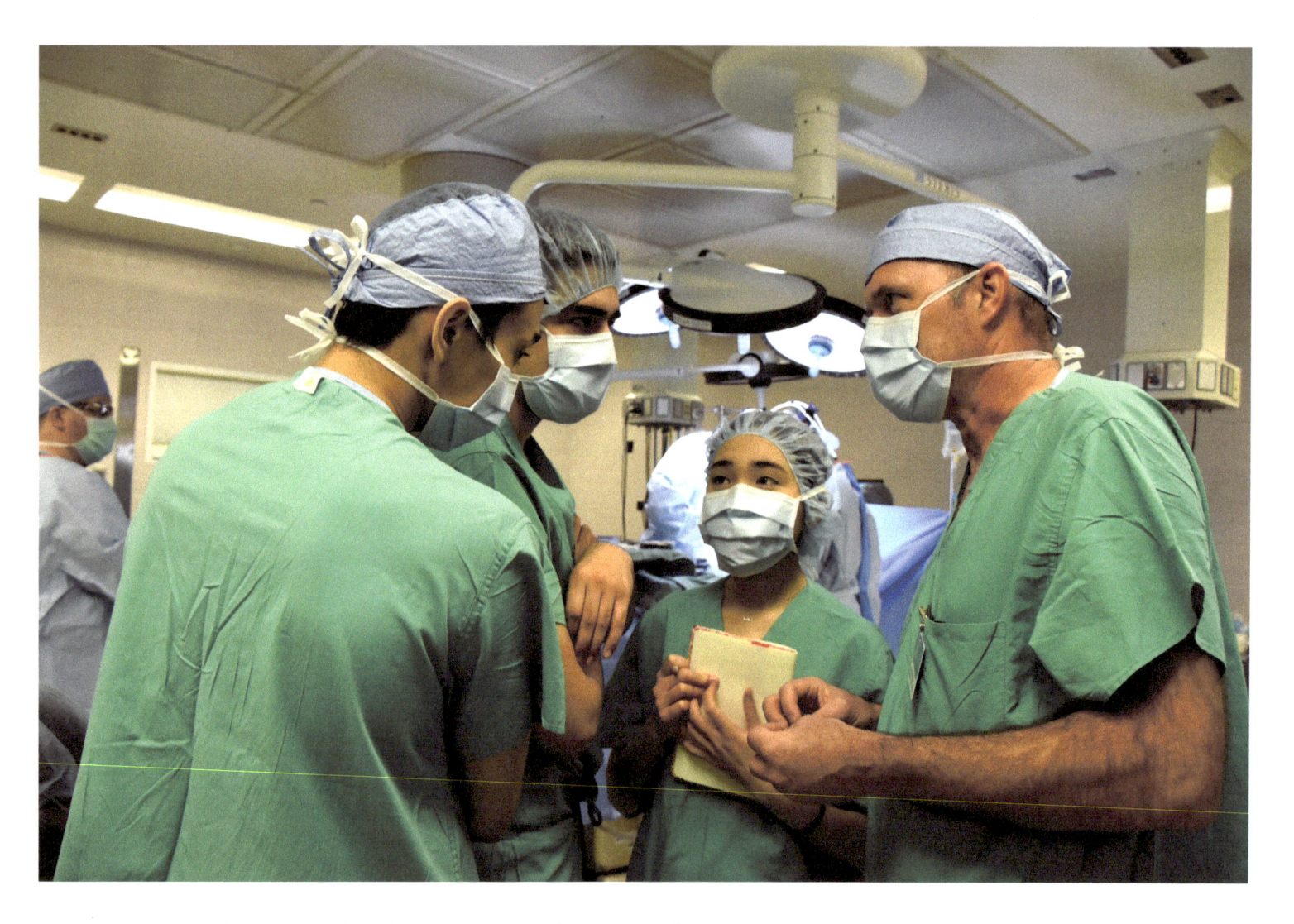

Virginia Tech and Carilion Clinic formed a public-private partnership in 2007 to create a new medical school and research institute. From this partnership came the Virginia Tech Carilion School of Medicine and Research Institute, which became an official college of Virginia Tech in 2018. This photo shows students in the Clinical Neuroscience in Practice course at Carilion Clinic in early 2017.

The Virginia Tech Carilion School of Medicine graduated its first class, shown here, in 2014.

The Virginia Tech Carilion Research Institute was renamed the Fralin Biomedical Research Institute at VTC in 2019, in recognition of a $50 million gift from the Horace G. Fralin Charitable Trust, and Heywood and Cynthia Fralin. A major milestone of the institute came in 2021 with the official opening of a $90 million addition, shown here, which dramatically increased the institute's capacity to take on the challenges of brain disorders, cardiovascular disease, cancer, metabolism and obesity, companion animal health, and infectious disease.

The Virginia Tech Corporate Research Center (CRC) was established in Blacksburg in 1985 as a place where Virginia Tech researchers could realize the commercial potential of their work. Over the years the CRC has been home to over 750 organizations, including Industrial Biodynamics, which began manufacturing a slip-and-fall simulator at CRC in 2014. Now used by major companies including UPS, FedEx, and DuPont to increase worker safety, the technology was first developed by a team of Virginia Tech researchers in the Grado Department of Industrial and Systems Engineering. The company is now headquartered in Salem, Virginia.

Since opening in 2000, Torgersen Hall, with its distinctive "Torg Bridge" reading room that spans Alumni Mall, has become one of the most recognizable landmarks on campus. The building is a fitting tribute to Virginia Tech's fourteenth president, Paul Torgersen, a revered educator who, even while he was president from 1994 to 2000 and dean of the College of Engineering from 1970 to 1990, taught at least one course per semester.

Located in Basel, Switzerland, in a villa more than 250 years old that was acquired by the Virginia Tech Foundation in 1992, the Steger Center for International Scholarship grew out of a desire for a permanent home for the College of Architecture and Urban Studies' study abroad program. Following renovations in 2014, the center offers housing, multipurpose and dining spaces, a subdividable classroom space, and support spaces for Virginia Tech students taking part in European study abroad experiences.

Since its opening in 2013, the Moss Arts Center has hosted hundreds of performances and exhibitions along with additional programing designed to engage both the campus and surrounding community. Shown here, legendary cellist Yo-Yo Ma leads a special master class in 2017 for students from the School of Performing Arts in the Anne and Ellen Fife Theatre, located in the Moss Arts Center's Street and Davis Performance Hall. The master class followed a sold-out performance by Ma and pianist Kathryn Stott the previous day.

The Institute for Creativity, Arts, and Technology (ICAT) hosts the Virginia Tech Science Festival, an annual expo-style event that showcases science education and research programs at the university. The festival features exhibits and "hands-on" activities like the one pictured here at the Moss Arts Center in 2017, making it popular both on campus and in the surrounding community.

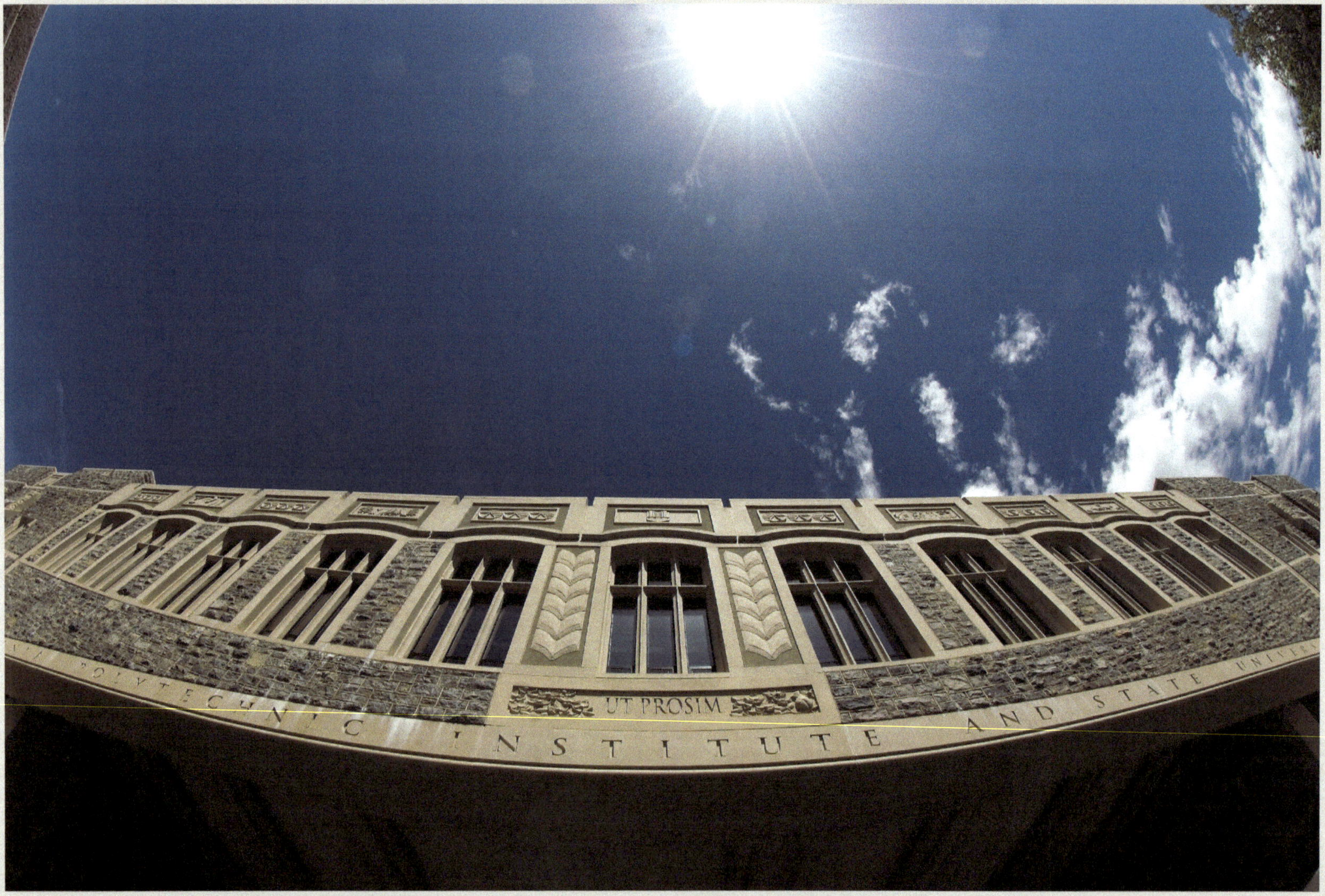
UT PROSIM
POLYTECHNIC INSTITUTE AND STATE

PART THREE

INNOVATION

VIRGINIA TECH'S DEEP ROOTS in the mechanical arts has fostered a unique culture of innovation that has continued into the present day. Faculty and students of the nineteenth, twentieth, and twenty-first centuries share the common goal of improving society through new inventions, processes, and approaches. It is not surprising, therefore, that an eagerness to tackle societal problems is a key part of what draws many students and faculty to Virginia Tech. Thinking outside the box is more than just a slogan; it is part of the collegiate experience.

This section focuses on some of the more recent innovative breakthroughs at Virginia Tech. Beginning with early efforts in space science, nuclear energy, and computer technology, the section documents such achievements as the Smart Road and the Virginia Tech Transportation Institute, the FutureHAUS (or smart house), biomedical research and health education programs, and the development of scalable drone delivery technology. Finally, this section features some of the most recent events in Virginia Tech's history, such as the response to the COVID-19 pandemic and the planned Innovation Campus in Northern Virginia. Within these images are hints of what the next 150 years at Virginia Tech will produce.

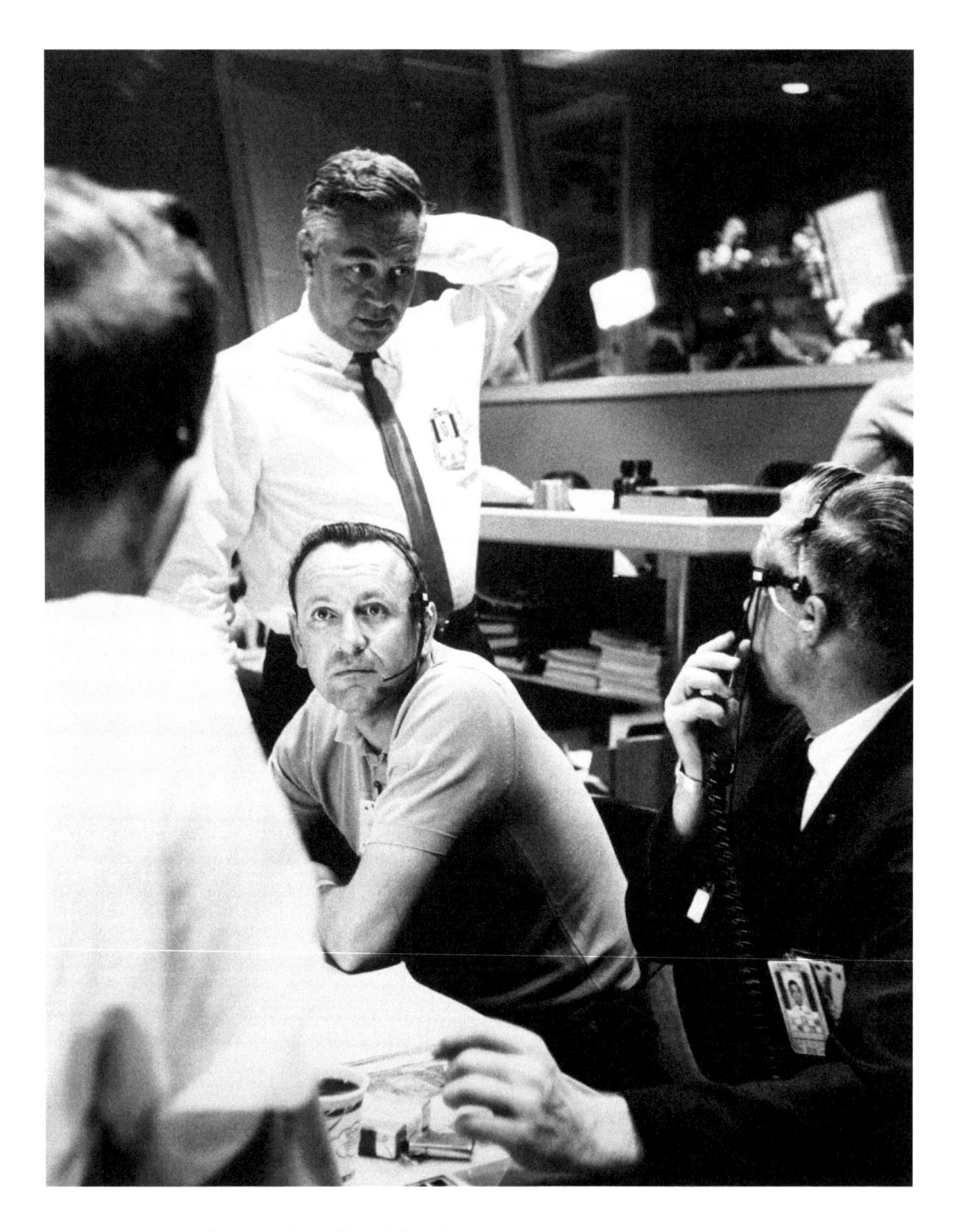

Christopher Kraft, founder of NASA's Mission Control, graduated from Virginia Tech in 1944 with a bachelor's degree in aeronautical engineering. Numerous Hokies have since worked for NASA, including Homer Hickam, author of *Rocket Boys*, who credits Kraft with making a name for Virginia Tech at NASA. This photo from 1963 shows Kraft (center) at his console in Cape Canaveral during the Mercury Atlas 9 mission as the decision is being made to go for the full 22 orbits. (NASA photo)

One sign of Kraft's legacy at Virginia Tech is the Center for Space Science and Engineering Research (Space@VT), where faculty, students, and staff from multiple scientific disciplines pursue research in space-related fields. By working on Space@VT projects, undergraduate and graduate students gain hands-on experience that prepares them for careers in the space industry, government labs, and academic institutions. The top photo shows students at a Space@VT workspace taking part in tracking satellites as they pass over Virginia during their orbit of the earth. At bottom, an undergraduate student collaborates with a graduate student on a Space@VT project.

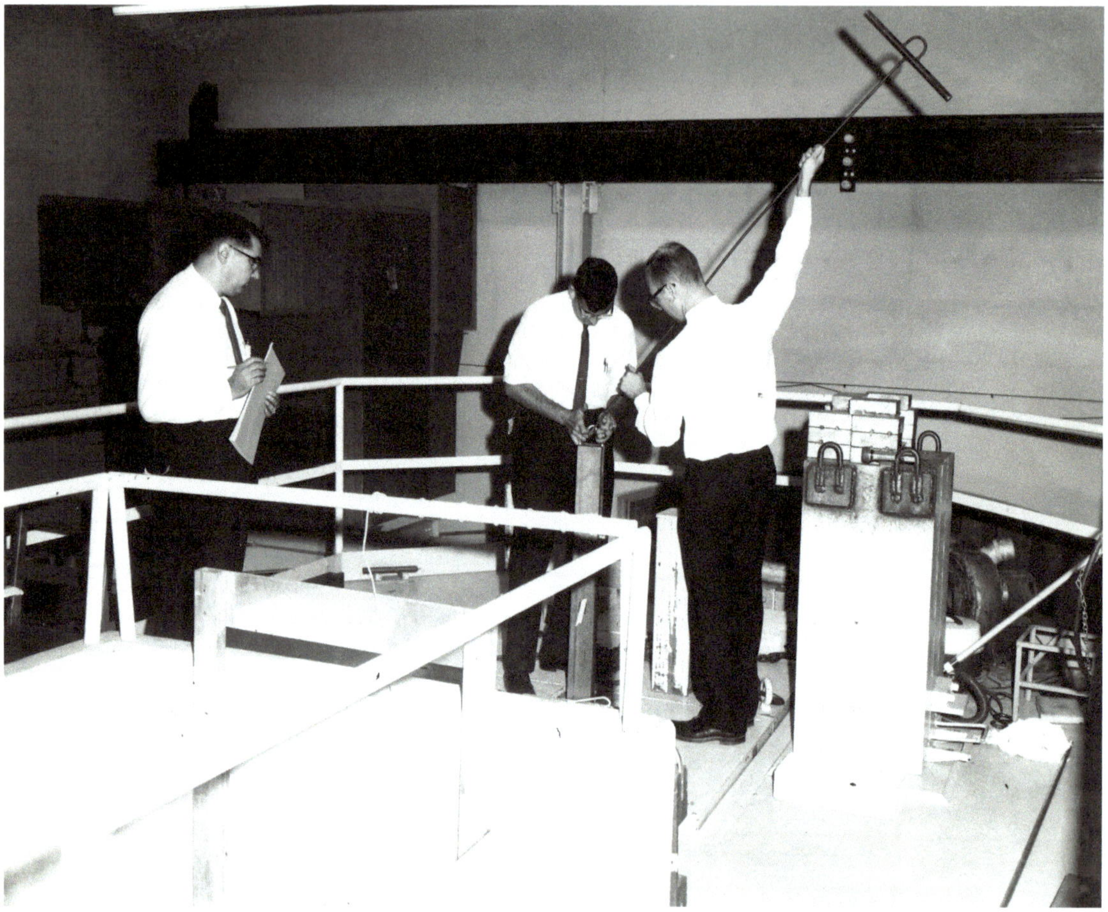

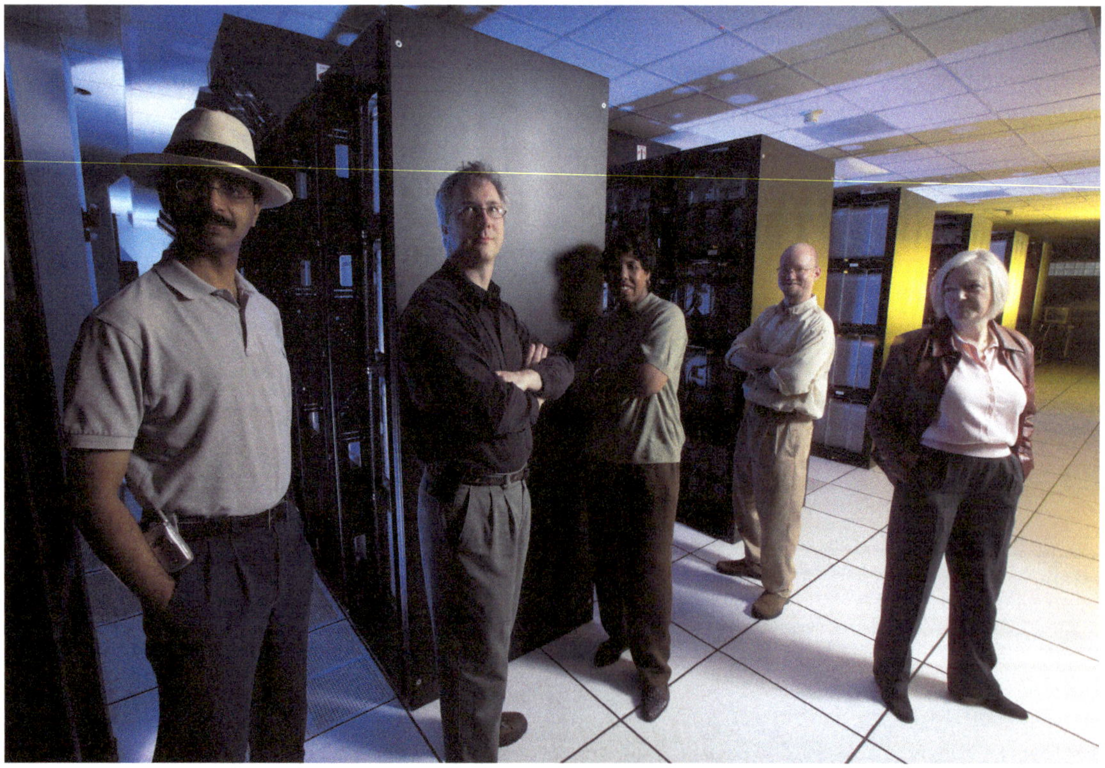

Researchers from Virginia Tech are developing humanoid robots that can perform complex tasks in a variety of real-world scenarios. In 2015 the Terrestrial Robotics Engineering & Controls Lab (TREC) brought its self-built robot ESCHER under the banner Team VALOR to the DARPA Robotics Challenge in Pomona, California. Here ESCHER wowed onlookers by walking untethered 200 feet along a loose dirt-covered path.

OPPOSITE TOP: From 1962 to 1981, Virginia Tech operated an Argonaut (Argonne Nuclear Assembly for University Training) 100-kilowatt nuclear reactor in Robeson Hall. Here two nuclear engineering and physics graduate students conduct an experiment on top of the reactor under a professor's supervision.

OPPOSITE BOTTOM: System X, Virginia Tech's first supercomputer, was assembled in summer 2003 by faculty, staff, and students for a mere $5.2 million, and at the time was ranked as the world's most powerful and cheapest homebuilt supercomputer. By comparison, the fastest supercomputer at that time cost approximately $400 million to build. System X was retired in 2012. Pictured are the project leads, left to right: Srinidhi Varadarajan, Kevin Shinbaugh, Glenda Scales, Jason Lockhart, and Pat Arvin.

Goodwin Hall, the flagship building for the College of Engineering, opened in June 2014 rigged with 241 accelerometers that measure motion and vibration inside and outside its walls. A major attraction of the building is the 14,000-pound Rolls Royce Trent 1000 jet engine hanging above the first-floor atrium. Donated by the London-based engine builder as a learning tool for engineering students, the engine was shipped from London to Baltimore, then driven to Blacksburg.

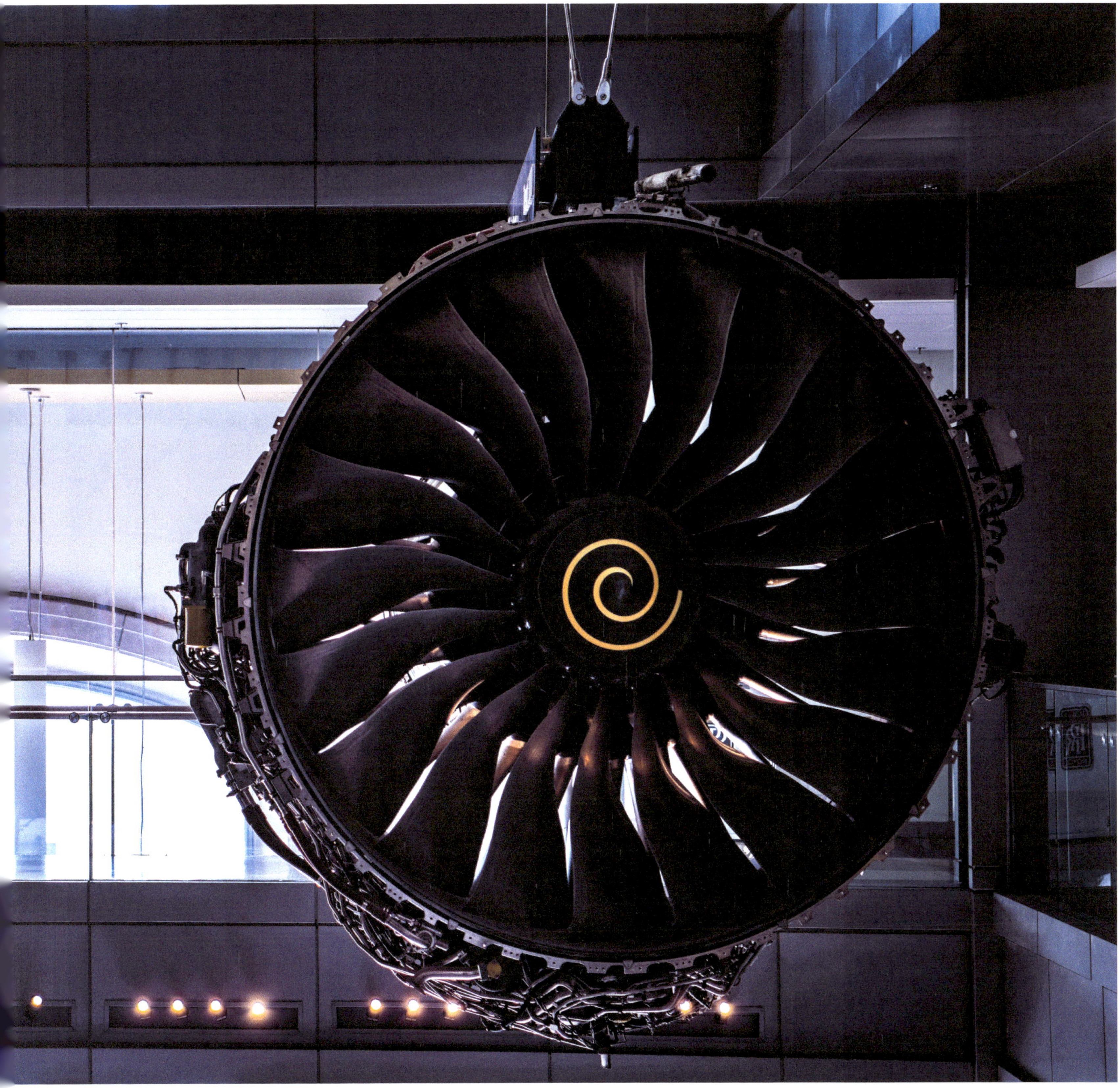

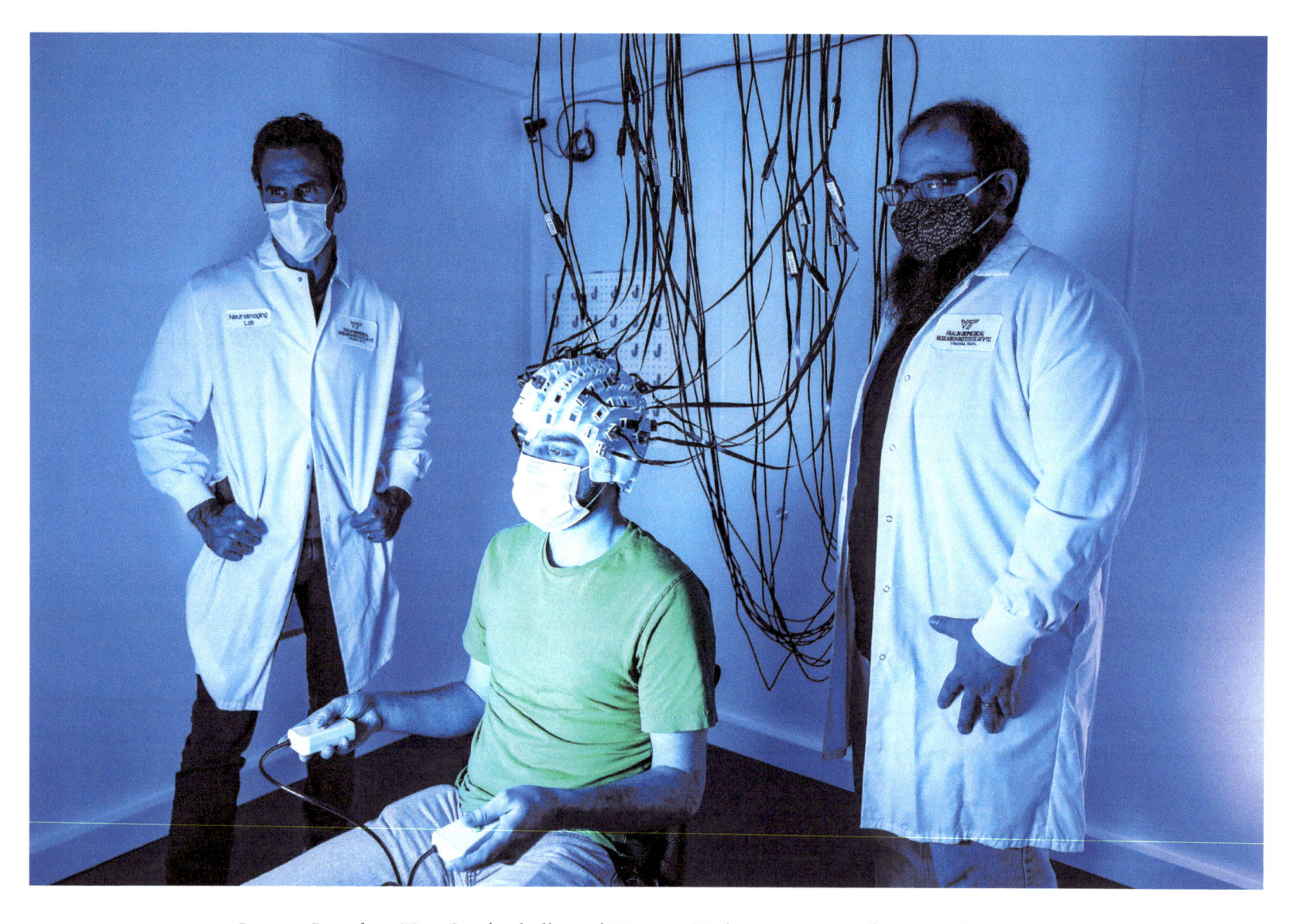

In 2015 President Tim Sands challenged Virginia Tech to envision a future without constraints of today's perspectives and perceived barriers. The result was the "Beyond Boundaries" initiative, an important piece of which is the concept of Destination Areas (DAs)—transdisciplinary communities that work collaboratively to address complex problems affecting the human condition. The next pages document a few of the DAs.

ABOVE: Researchers associated with the Adaptive Brain and Behavior DA demonstrate the use of optically pumped magnetometry technology at the Center for Human Neuroscience Research in the Fralin Biomedical Research Institute at Virginia Tech Carilion.

TOP: The Integrated Security DA is committed to fostering a world in which individuals, institutions, and nations are secured by technology and social systems that follow ethical principles and promote values of social justice. Here, students in an Integrated Security course discuss a response for mock cyberattacks and natural disasters.

BOTTOM: Blockchain technology has applications that span multiple DAs. In 2018 the Department of Computer Science launched its Blockchain @ VT initiative with funding from Block.one. This photo is from the 2018 Blacksburg Blockchain Symposium, hosted by Virginia Tech's Global Forum on Urban and Regional Resilience.

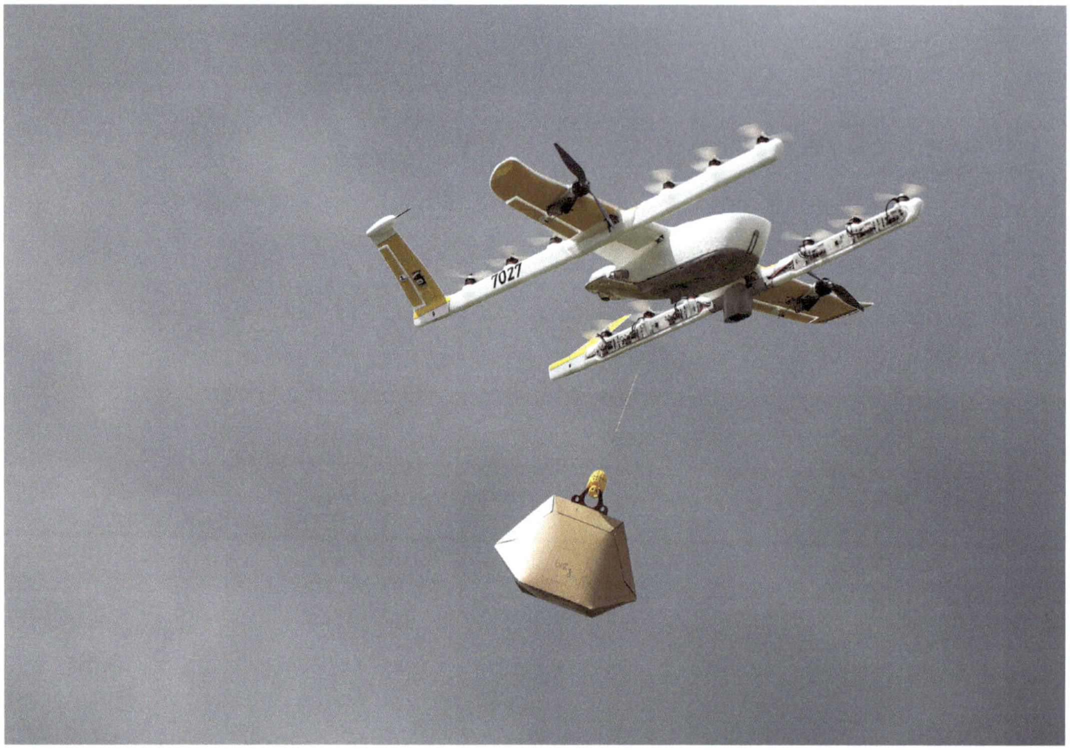
7027

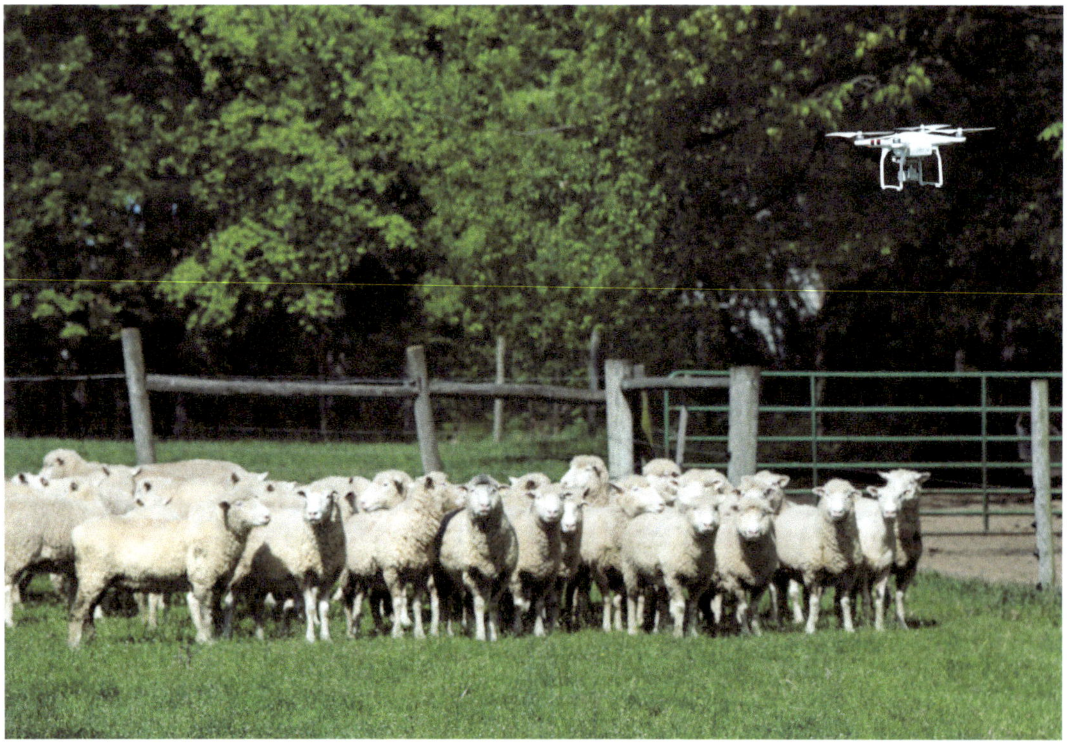

Virginia Tech has been a leader in the development of unmanned aircraft systems (UAS). Above, President Sands speaks at the opening of the Virginia Tech Drone Park in 2018. The facility gives university and community members a place to explore UAS operations without the constraints of registration, certification, or specialized training.

OPPOSITE: Two examples of Virginia Tech's varied work with UAS technology: The top photo shows a drone delivering popsicles and ice cream to two homes in Montgomery County as part of a partnership between the Virginia Tech Mid-Atlantic Aviation Partnership (MAAP) and Wing, an offshoot of Google. At bottom, a drone monitors sheep at the Copenhaver Sheep Center—one way the College of Agriculture and Life Sciences is helping Virginia farmers deploy innovative technologies to increase efficiency, resilience, and sustainability.

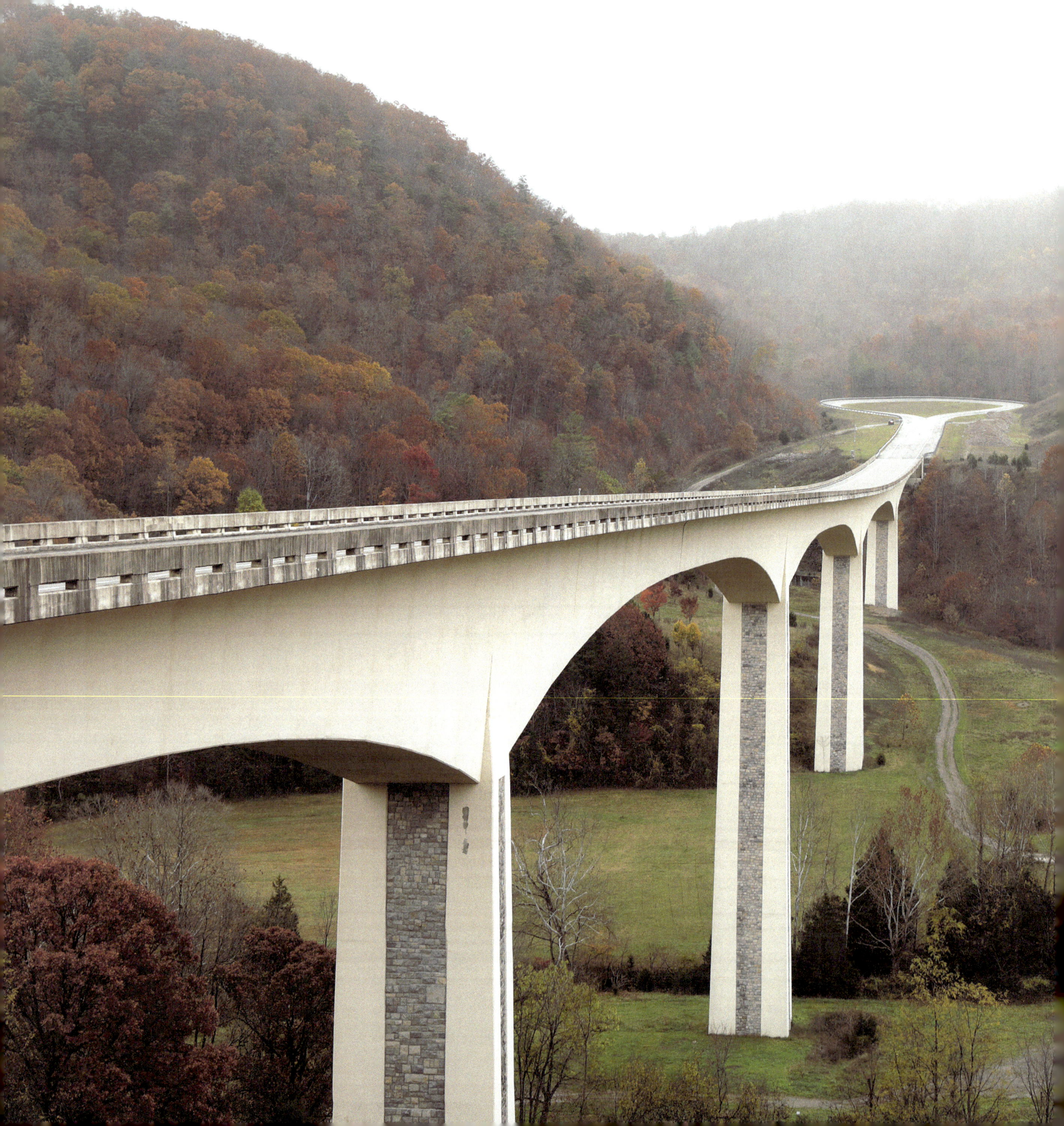

The Virginia Tech Transportation Institute (VTTI), one of the largest of its kind at an American university, conducts research devoted to finding safety-first, data-based solutions to national and global transportation challenges. In partnership with VDOT, VTTI opened the original Virginia Smart Road in 2000. Since then, more smart roads have been added that enable advanced-vehicle testing. VTTI has also been at the forefront of autonomous vehicle research (BELOW). In 2019 the U.S. Department of Transportation announced two grants to VTTI, totaling $15 million to advance research on the safe integration of automation into U.S. roadways.

Virginia Tech's Center for Design Research, which brings together students and faculty from multiple colleges, has been exploring the architecture and engineering of energy positive housing for more than two decades. In 2010 the Center's LumenHAUS team won the inaugural Solar Decathlon Europe competition in Madrid, Spain.

In 2018 the Center for Design Research brought home first place in the Solar Decathlon Middle East competition in Dubai for FutureHAUS, shown here being installed in Times Square, New York City, May 9, 2019.

The Cube is a unique four-story-high theatre and high-tech laboratory space, located in the Moss Arts Center, that accommodates everything from intimate performances and audio and visual installations to research and experimentation in big data applications and testing of immersive environments. A joint venture of Moss and ICAT, the Cube is a centerpiece of the Creativity + Innovation DA where faculty and students from across Virginia Tech can explore the integration of the arts, business, design, humanities, and technology.

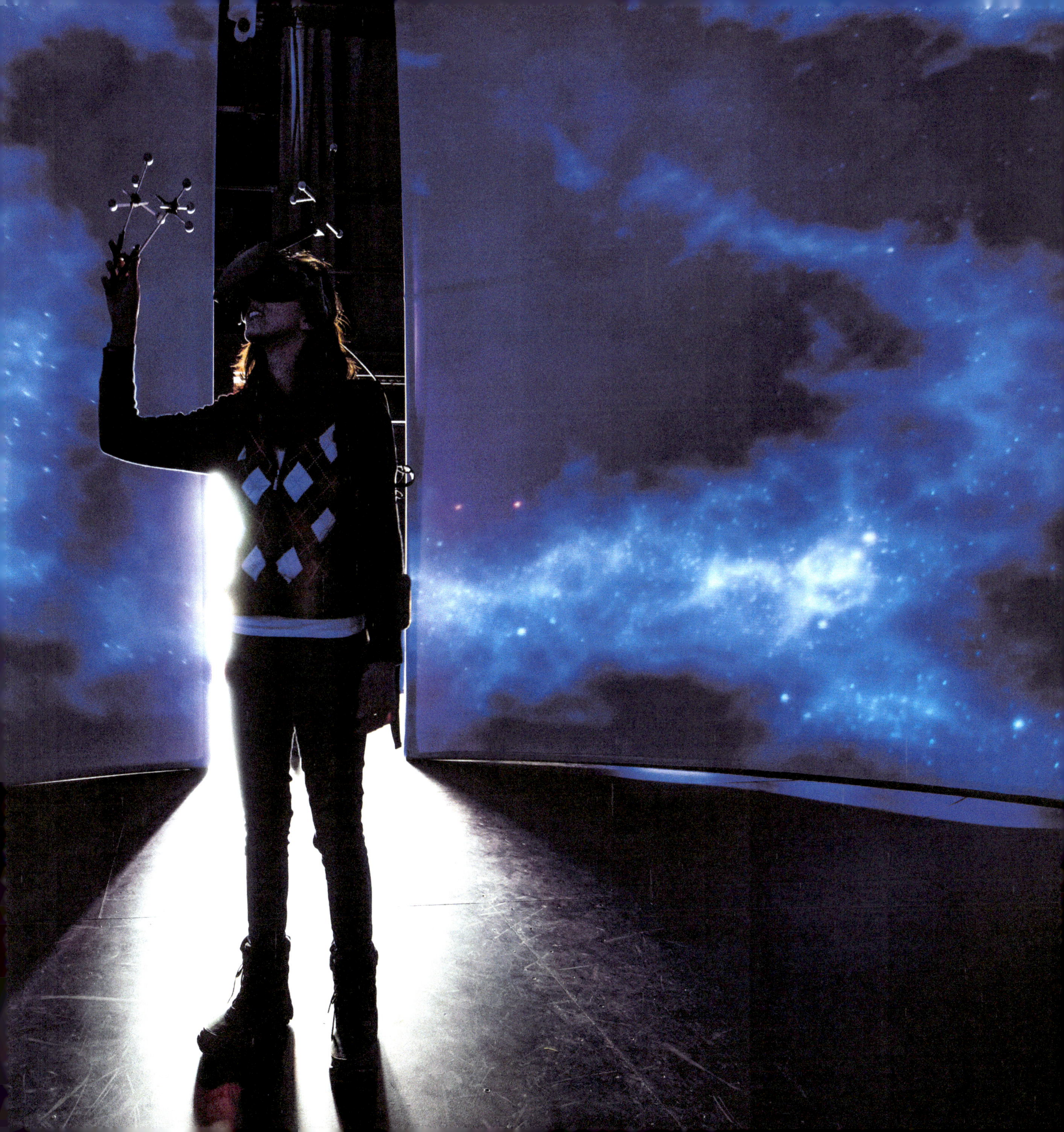

The launch of the Center for Humanities in 2017 was an indication of how the humanities at Virginia Tech have become more integrated across colleges, with human and social sciences providing insight into how technology, engineering, medical science, and other areas can be more person-focused as well as equitable and inclusive. Shown here is Sylvester Johnson, founding director of the Center for Humanities, speaking with students in Newman Library.

Marc Edwards worked with dozens of students and faculty from Virginia Tech and collaborated with Lee-Anne Walters, Mona Hanna-Attisha, and other residents and activists on the Flint, Michigan, Water Study Team to identify poisonous levels of lead in their tap water. One resident, Elnora Carthan (left), is shown with Edwards after new pipes were installed in her home in 2016.

INNOVATION CAMPUS
VIRGINIA TECH
vt.edu
Fostering collaboration in a strategic location.
INNOVATION CAMPUS

Virginia Tech and Qualcomm began a multiyear collaboration in 2016 with the launch of the Qualcomm Thinkabit Lab at the Virginia Tech Northern Virginia Center in Falls Church. The lab offers K-12 students from Northern Virginia and DC area schools a hands-on experience in science, technology, engineering, and math while raising awareness of possible future careers. Here middle-school students build a "Robo Craft" with electronic equipment, including laptop computers, Arduinos, servos, resisters, circuits, LEDs, breadboards, and solar panels.

OPPOSITE: Plans for the Virginia Tech Innovation Campus were announced in November 2018 as part of the Commonwealth of Virginia's successful bid to attract Amazon's HQ2 to Northern Virginia. The new campus, to be located in the Potomac Yard area of Alexandria, will focus on graduate education in computer science and computer engineering with a project-based approach to learning that links industry, government, and academia. The top photo shows Lance R. Collins, the inaugural vice president and executive director of the Innovation Campus, in the temporary campus headquarters in Alexandria. Behind him can be seen a rendering of the first Innovation Campus building, set to open in 2024. The bottom photo is from the groundbreaking ceremony for that building in September 2021.

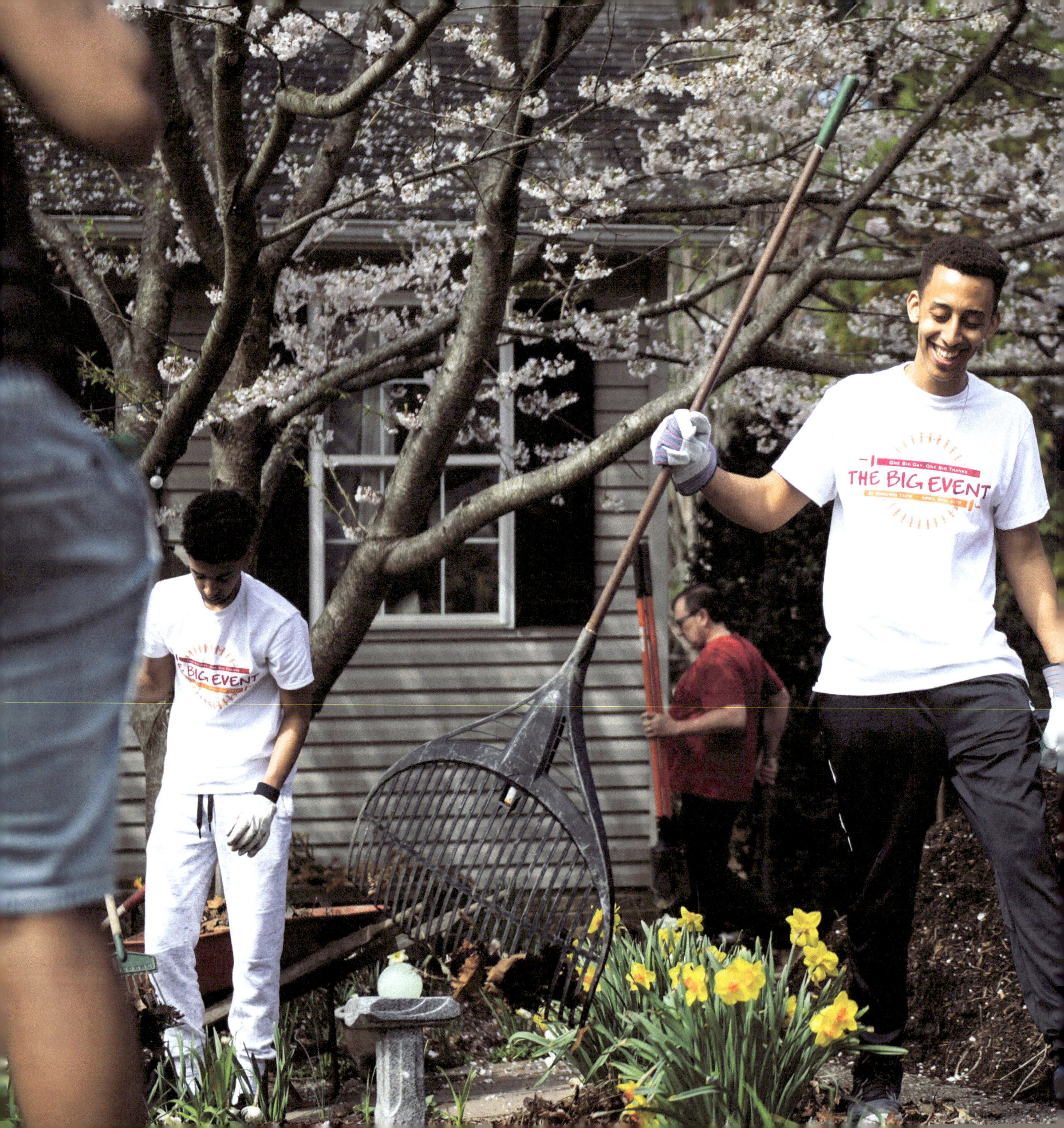
One Big Day. One Big Thanks
THE BIG EVENT

The spirit of *Ut Prosim* continues through student-sponsored service activities and charitable events including Shacksburg, where teams build temporary structures to raise funds for Habitat for Humanity, and Relay for Life, which promotes awareness and raises donations for the American Cancer Society. The Big Event is an annual student-run day of service, the second largest of its kind in the U.S., where students, faculty, staff, and community members take part in service projects in the New River Valley.

Virginia Tech researchers have been instrumental in addressing all aspects of the COVID-19 pandemic. Linsey Marr (TOP) and her civil and environmental engineering students studied the efficacy of N95 respirators, and Marr became a public voice explaining the transmission and prevention of infectious diseases like COVID-19. Carla Finkielstein (BOTTOM), who leads the VTC Fralin Biomedical Research Institute's Molecular Diagnostics Laboratory, has worked to develop a reliable qRT-PCR-based assay.

COVID-19 changed the way everyone at Virginia Tech worked, studied, and socialized. As more became known about the virus, safety protocols for preventing transmission were put in place across campus. In October 2020 the College of Architecture and Urban Studies built a 2,900-square-foot geodesic dome outside Cowgill Hall to provide additional space for faculty teaching, student pin-ups, and small gatherings.

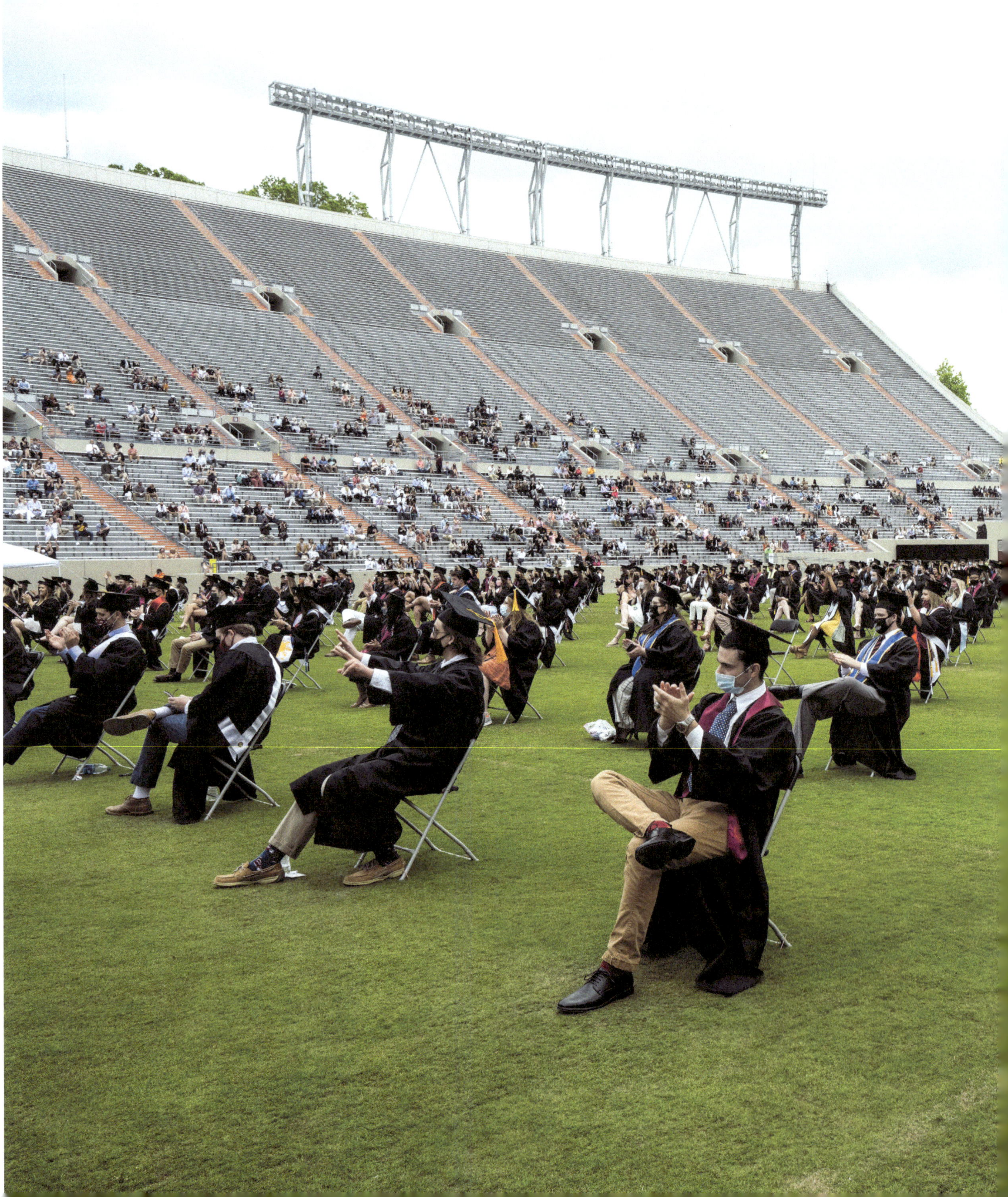

After COVID-19 upended spring commencement plans in 2020, in-person ceremonies returned to campus in 2021, albeit in modified form. This photo is from the College of Science ceremony at Lane Stadium on May 14, 2021.

Virginia Tech's Animal-Assisted Therapy program at Cook Counseling Center has gained a national reputation for its innovative approach to breaking down mental wellness stigmas. The program started in 2013 with golden Labrador retriever Moose, who aided in more than 7,500 counseling sessions and more than 500 outreach events during his seven years at Tech before he died in 2020. Here Moose and his fellow therapy dog Derek pose for the camera at the 2019 Homecoming Parade with Hokie Camille Schrier '18 before she was crowned Miss America 2020.

FURTHER READING

Cox, Clara B. and Jenkins M. Robertson, "Historical Digest," https://history.unirel.vt.edu/historical_digest.html.

Harris, Nelson. *Virginia Tech*. Charleston, S.C.: Arcadia, 2004.

Hinker, Lawrence G., and Clara B. Cox, eds. *Images & Reflections: Virginia Tech, 1872-1997*. Blacksburg: VPI in conjunction with Harmony House Publishers, 1997.

Kinnear, Duncan Lyle. *The First 100 Years: A History of Virginia Polytechnic Institute and State University*. Blacksburg: VPI, 1972.

Morozov, Ivan (photographer). *Virginia Tech: A Pictorial Tour*. Blacksburg: Ivan Morozov, 2012.

Shoffner, Charles (photographer). *Then and Now: Virginia Tech*. Louisville: Harmony House, 1991.

Strother, Warren H., and Peter Wallenstein. *From VPI to State University: President T. Marshall Hahn, Jr. and the Transformation of Virginia Tech, 1962-1974*. Macon, Ga.: Mercer University Press, 2004.

Temple, Harry Downing. *The Bugle's Echo: A Chronology of Cadet Life at the Military College at Blacksburg, Virginia, the Virginia Agricultural and Mechanical College, and the Virginia Polytechnic Institute*. 6 vols. Blacksburg: Virginia Tech Corps of Cadets Alumni, Inc., 1996-2001.

Tillar, Thomas C. Jr., ed. *Tech Triumph: A Pictorial History of Virginia Tech*. Blacksburg: Virginia Tech Alumni Association, 1984.

Wallenstein, Peter. *Virginia Tech, Land-Grant University, 1872-1997: History of a School, a State, a Nation*. Blacksburg: Pocahontas Press, 1997; Second edition. Blacksburg: Virginia Tech Publishing, 2022.

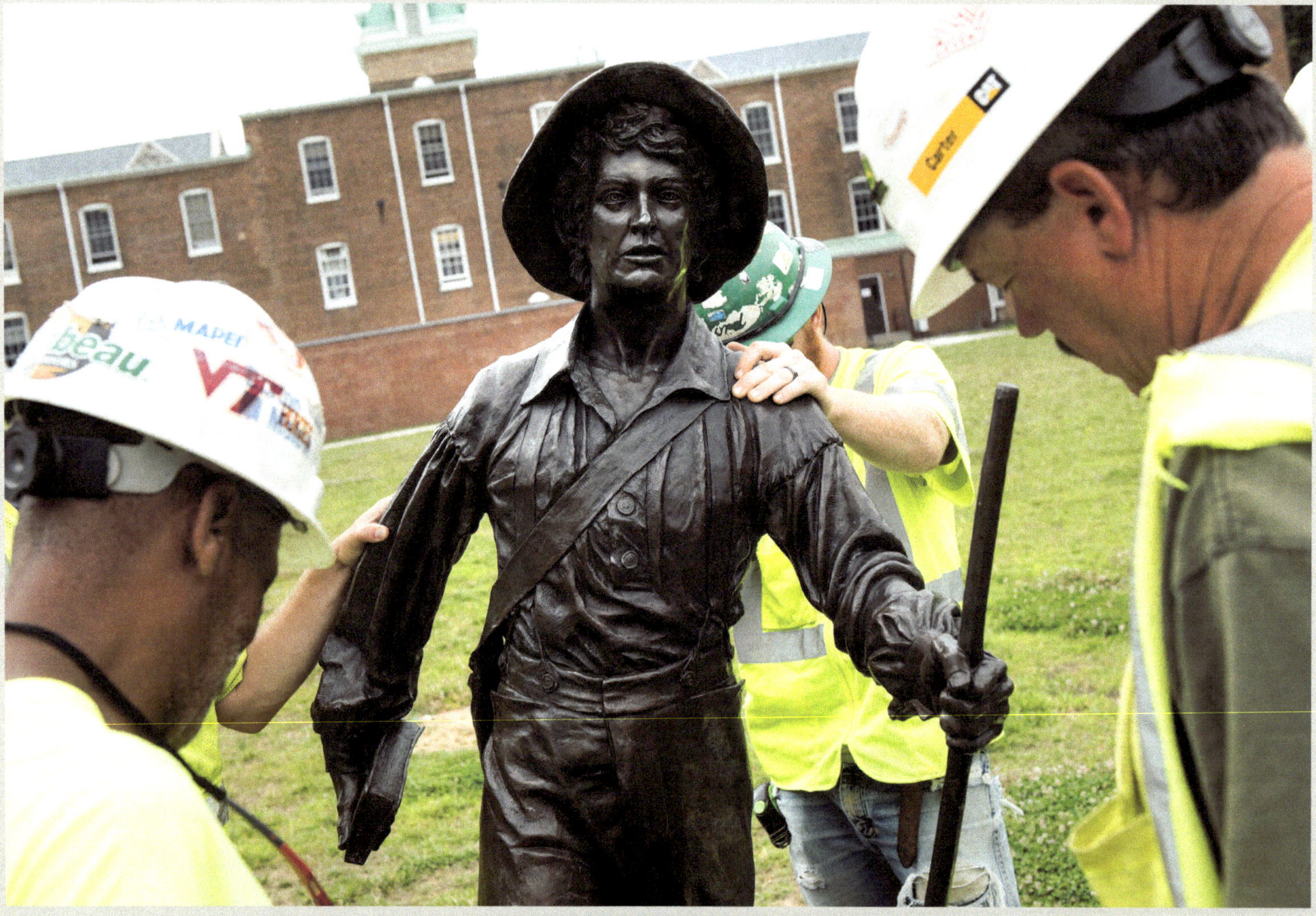
beau
Carter

ABOUT THE AUTHORS

AARON D. PURCELL is Director of Special Collections and University Archives at Virginia Tech. He previously worked at the University of Tennessee, the National Library of Medicine, and the National Archives and Records Administration. Purcell has written several books in the fields of archives and history.

LM ROZEMA is Processing and Special Projects Archivist at Virginia Tech. She previously worked at the Dolph Briscoe Center for American History at the University of Texas at Austin.

ANTHONY WRIGHT DE HERNANDEZ is Community Collections Archivist at Virginia Tech.

JOHN M. JACKSON is a library specialist at Virginia Tech. He previously worked at the University of Arkansas at Little Rock. Jackson has edited two books relating to the history of West Virginia.

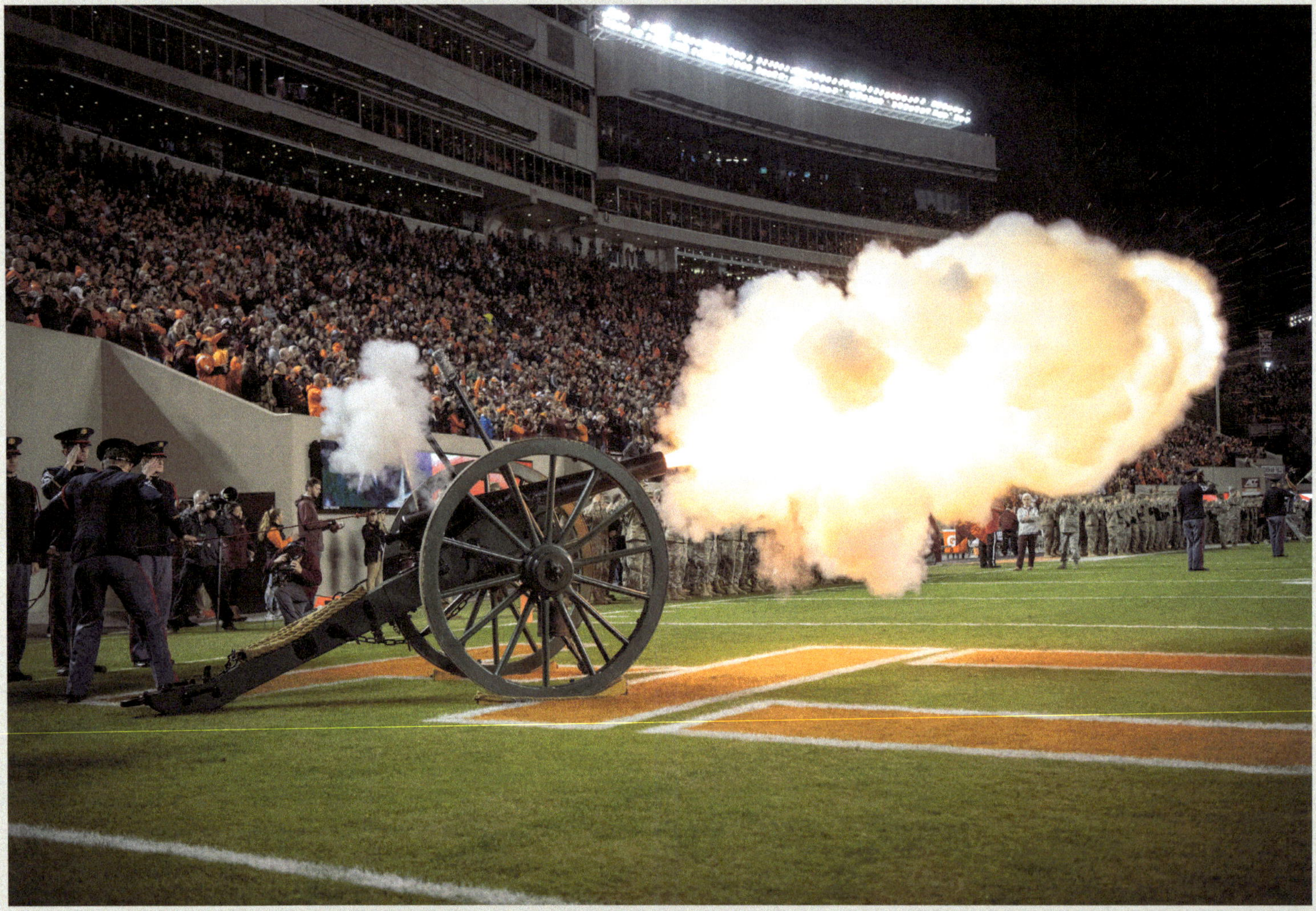

INDEX

Adams, Linda, 15
Agnew, Ella Graham, 10, 45
Agricultural Research and Extension Centers (ARECs), 138
Alumni Gateway, 68
Alumni Mall, 22, 32, 96, 146
American Cancer Society, 173
American Indian and Indigenous Community Center, 105
Animal Cancer Care and Research Center, 140
April 16, 2007, 22, 134, 135, 136-37
Arbery, Ahmaud, 25
Argonaut (Argonne Nuclear Assembly for University Training), 154-55
Army Specialized Training Program, 13, 77
Arvin, Pat, 154-55
Asian Cultural Engagement Center, 105
Asian people, 15, 62, 105
athletics; baseball, 121; football, 20, 35, 36, 118-19, 120, 121, 122-23, 124; men's basketball, 19, 124-25; Olympians, 124, 128-29; recreational and intermural sports, 20, 130-33; tennis, 132; track and field, 128-29; Virginia Tech Sports Hall of Fame, 126-27, women's basketball, 19-20, 126-127
Atlantic Coast Conference (ACC), 19, 20, 124, 129
Avrum Gudelsky Veterinary Medicine Center, 140

bands, vi, 36
Barracks No. 1, 8, 33, 34, 51, 54, 94
Barracks No. 2, 33, 54
Barringer Hall, 25, 107
Beamer, Frank, 20, 124

Beyond Boundaries, 23, 158
Big Event, 172-73
Black Cultural Center, 105, 115
Black Faculty and Staff Caucus, 111
Black Organizations Council, 106-107
Black people; admission to Virginia Tech, ix, 15-16, 25, 80-81, 96; alumni reunions, 81, 111; and athletics, 124-25, 126-27, 128-29; and Black Cultural Center, 105, 115; and Black Lives Matter, 106-107; and building names, 24-25, 81, 107; enslaved African people at Smithfield and Solitude, 2, 29; faculty and staff at Virginia Tech, 15, 34, 80, 111, 118, 136-37; first graduates, 15, 80-81; and higher education funding, 2; and homecoming, 116-17; and Virginia Cooperative Extension, 67; and Virginia Tech Corps of Cadets, 80, 96
Black, William, 92
Black Lives Matter, 106-107
Blacksburg; and the Agricultural Experiment Station, 8; and the Blacksburg Electronic Village, 19; early history, 92; and the Huckleberry Railroad, 41; mentioned, 42, 68, 69, 70, 93, 133, 156, 159; and the Smart Road, 19; and the Virginia Tech campus, 2, 4, 6, 14, 18, 20, 22, 27, 98, 140, 145
Blacksburg Electronic Village, 19
Blair, Marion Buford, 126
Blockchain, 159
Boggs, W.R., 30
Brumfield, Mary E., 12, 60
Buchanan, John Lee, 7
Bugle, 9, 24, 59
Burruss, Julian A., 12
Burruss Hall, 77, 88, 90, 134

183

Bush, George W., 137
Butler, Dave, 135
Butler, Jacquelyn, 15

Caldwell, William Addison, xiv, 6, 31, 180
Campbell, Anna, 13
Carilion Clinic, 20, 88, 142, 143, 144, 158
Carroll, Gray, 30
Carthan, Elnora, 169
Cassell Coliseum, 137
Castlin, Kristi, 129
Center for Design Research, 164, 165
Center for Human Neuroscience Research, 158
Center for Humanities, 168
Center for Space Science and Engineering Research (Space@VT), 153
Christiansburg, 19, 41
Civil War, 1, 4
Coffey, Charlie, 119
Coles, Venell Eufaye "Bimbo," 124–25
Collegiate Times, 86
Collins, Lance R., 170–71
Color War, 112
Commencement Hall, 32
commencements, xi, 6, 25, 88-89, 176–77
Commerce Hall, 74
Conrad, Thomas Nelson, 7–8
Cook Counseling Center, 178
Coordinating Council for Women's Concerns, 104
Copenhaver Sheep Center, 161
Council of International Student Organizations, 108–109, 112
Council on Virginia Tech History, 24–25
COVID-19, 24, 151, 174, 175, 176–77
Cowgill Hall, 175
Cranwell International Center, 112
Creativity and Innovation District (CID), 22–23
Cube, the, 22, 166-67
Cultural and Community Centers, 105

Cyrus McCormick Farm, 79
Darden, Colgate W., Jr., 14
Davidson Hall, 76–77, 78
Davis, Mary Moore, 45
Day of Remembrance, 134
Denim Day, 100–101
Dennis, Renee, 126
Destination Areas, 23, 158, 159, 166
Dietrick Hall, 111
Digging in the Crates, 114–15
Dodd, Lauren, 141
Doss, L.J., 82
Drillfield, 12, 14, 52, 75, 77, 78, 85
Duck Pond, 15, 71, 78
Dunsmuir, James, 14
Duvall, Roger, 86–87

Edmonds, Linda, 15
Edward Via College of Osteopathic Medicine, 20
Edwards, Marc, 169
El Centro (Hispanic and Latinx Cultural and Community Center), 105
Electronic Theses and Dissertations, 19
Elliott, Rufus, 16
Ellzey, M.G., 30
Eppes, Mattie, 57

Faculty Row, 9, 52
Felder, Marva, 116–17
Finkielstein, Carla, 174
Floyd, George, 25
Founders Day, 17
4-H, 45, 67, 138
Fraction family, 2, 29
Fralin, Cynthia, 144
Fralin, Heywood, 144
Fralin, Horace C., 144
Fralin Biomedical Research Institute, 20, 144, 158, 174
Fralin Life Sciences Institute, 20
Fung, Tek Heung, 62

Future Farmers of America, 12, 66
Future Famers of Virginia, 12, 66
FutureHAUS, 151, 165

Gay Alliance of Virginia Tech, 113
Gay Student Alliance, 100-101, 113
G.I. Bill, 14, 78
Giovanni, Nikki, 136–37
Global Forum on Urban and Regional Resilience, 159
Gobblers and Fighting Gobblers, 9, 19, 35, 83, 118–19
Godwin, Mills E., Jr., 83
Goodwin Hall, 156–57
Gray Jacket, 74
Gregory, Earle D., 12
Groseclose, Henry C., 66
Grove, the, 8

Habitat for Humanity, 173
Hahn, T. Marshall, 16–17, 18, 83, 98
Hairston, LaVerne, 15
Hampton University, 2, 80
Harnett, Jason, 132–33
Harper, Marguerite, 15
Harrison-Claye, Queen, 120
Henderson Hall, 32
Hickam, Homer, 152
Highty-Tighties, 36, 97
Hillcrest Hall, 13
Hi-Techs, 119
Hoge family, 25, 80
Hoge Hall, 25, 107
Hokie cheer, 10
Hokie nickname, 1, 10, 19, 119
Hokie stone, v, 8, 52, 84–85
HokieBird mascot, 19, 118–19, 170
homecoming events, 113, 116–17, 178
Hotel Roanoke, 19
Huckleberry Railroad, 41
Hudson, Chiquita, 15

Hutcheson, John Redd, 40–41
Ice Pond, 71
Indian Students Association, 112
Indigenous people, 1, 2, 16, 105, 110
Institute for Creativity, Arts, and Technology (ICAT), 166
Intercultural Engagement Center, 105
International Street Fair, 112
international students, 14–15, 61, 62

Jacobs, Louise, 60
James Madison University, 12
Johnson, Overton R., 111
Johnson, Sylvester, 168

Kabrich, Billie Kent, 12
Kaine, Tim, 137
Kent State University, 98
Kentland, 19
Kraft, Christopher, 152, 153

Lancaster, Lucy Lee, 12, 60,
land-grant mission, ix, 1–2, 4, 25, 27, 69, 86
Lane, James H., 6–7, 30, 33, 94
Lane Hall, viii, 8, 33, 34, 51, 94–95
Lane Stadium, vi, 83, 122–23, 176–77
Latinx people, 61, 105, 117
Lavery William Edward, 19, 140
Lee, Cato, 15
Lee, Cladius Lee, 24
Lee Hall, 24, 25
Leich, Chester, 68
LGBTQ+ people, 100–101, 102, 103, 105, 113
LGBTQA+ Community at Virginia Tech (LGBTQ+ Resource Center), 105
libraries, 72–73
Lincoln, Abraham, 1
Litton-Reaves Hall, 66
Living-Learning Communities, 23, 80–81
Lockhart, Jason, 154–55
Lomax, Lundford Lindsay, 8

Lower Quad, 47–48
LumenHAUS, 164
Luster and Black Hardware Company, 70
Lybrook Row, 78

Ma, Yo-Yo, 148
MacPherson, Mercer, 118
Maddux, Wilfred P., 57
Magill, Edmund, 66
Marion duPont Scott Equine Medical Center, 140
Marr, Linsey, 174
Marr, R.A., 53
Martin, Charles, 30
Math Emporium, 19
McBryde, James Bolton, 38
McBryde, John McLaren, 8–9, 10, 37
McBryde, Mary Comfort, 38
McBryde Hall, 52, 100
Meade, Floyd "Hard Times," 118
Miles, Clarence P. "Sally," 121
Miles Field and Stadium, 120–21, 122
Military Laboratory Building, 68
Minor, Charles Landon Carter, 4, 6, 7, 30, 91
Monacan people, 2, 16
Montgomery County, 2, 17, 85, 161
"Moonlight and VPI," 75
Morrill Act, 1–2
Moss Arts Center, 22, 28, 88, 101, 148, 149, 166–67

Native at Virginia Tech, 110
Newman, Walter S., 66
Newman Library, 73, 168
Nita, Mizuho, 139
Norfolk and Western Railway, 41

Obama, Michelle, 88–89
Overseas Club, 57
Overton R. Johnson Step Show, 111
Owens, Charles, 34

Pearson Hall East, 57
Pearson Hall West, 57
Peddrew, Irving L., III, 15, 80–81
Peddrew-Yates Hall, 81
Prairie Quad, 121
Preston and Olin Institute, 2, 4, 6, 7, 28, 32
Preston family, 2, 29
Price, William Byrd "Joe Chesty," 118
Price Hall, 50–51
Professional Development Network, 19

Qualcomm Thinkabit Lab, 171

Radford Ordnance Works, 13
Radford University, 14, 16
Readjuster Party, 7
Relay for Life, 173
Ring Dance, 75
Roanoke, 19, 20, 88, 140, 141
Roanoke College, 121
Robeson Hall, 155
Rock House, 48
Rock, The, 57

Sanders, Harry W., 66
Sands, Timothy D., 24, 91, 101, 158, 161
Sandy, Thomas O., 10, 44
Scales, Glenda, 154–55
Schrier, Camille, 178
Science Building, 48
Sewanee University, 4
Shacksburg, 173
Shenandoah Valley Agricultural Research and Extension Center, 79
Shepherd, V.E., 30
Shinbaugh, Kevin, 154–55
Short Wave Club, 61
Sibold, Carrie T., 12, 60
"Skipper," 182
Smart Road, 19, 151, 162–63
Smithfield, 2, 92
snowball fight, 54
Snyder, Peter C., 94

Solitude, 2, 4, 29
Squires Student Center, 86, 105, 114–15
Steger, Charles, 88, 137
Steger Center for International Scholarship, 19, 147
Stott, Kathryn, 148
Stroubles Creek, 71
student protests, 16, 17, 98–99, 102, 103, 107
Stull, O.M., 10
System X, 154–55

Taylor, Breonna, 25
"Tech Triumph," 56–57
Terrestrial Robotics Engineering and Controls Lab (TREC), 155
Terrett, Ruth Louise, 12, 60, 126
Tin Horn, 12
Torgerson, Paul, 146
Torgerson Hall, 146
Tutelo people, 2

University of Chicago, 12
University of Mary Washington, 14
University of Maryland, 4
University of Missouri, 107
University of South Carolina, 8
University of Tennessee, 8
University of Virginia, 2, 4, 8, 14, 120–21
Upper Quad, 8, 33, 38, 57, 94
Ut Prosim, 1, 9, 14, 25, 27, 37, 82, 173

Varadarajan, Srinidhi, 154–55
Velez, Desiree, 117
Venegas, Carmen, 61
Vietnam War, 17, 82, 98–99
Virginia Agricultural Experiment Station, 8, 64, 79
Virginia Cooperative Extension, ix, 10, 17, 27, 44, 45, 46–47, 67, 138, 139
Virginia Department of Transportation, 163
Virginia-Maryland College of Veterinary Medicine (VMCVM), 20, 140, 141

Virginia Military Institute, 2, 7
Virginia State Fair, 65
Virginia State University, 2, 138
Virginia Tech, The, 86
Virginia Tech,
  Board of Visitors; and admission of women, 12; early history of, 4, 7, 8, 29, 30; and Hahn reorganization plans, 16–17, 18; And Hokie Stone, 85; and McBryde reorganization plans, 8, 10; and renaming buildings, 24–25, 81, 107; and Virginia Tech Principles of Community, 21–22, 102, 103
  Carilion School of Medicine, 20, 88, 142, 143
  Central Steam Plant, 43
  Corporate Research Center, 18, 145
  Corps of Cadets; and Barracks No. 1 (Lane Hall), 8, 33, 94; and Black cadets, 80, 96; and the "Caldwell March," 6; and the Highty-Tighties, 36; mentioned, viii, 14, 17, 31, 34, 41, 78, 91, 95; and military service, 12, 13–14, 57, 63, 77, 82; military training requirement, 6–7, 12, 16, 30, 83; and "Rat Parade," 62; and service to the community, 70; and "Skipper," 182; and snowball fight, 54; and women cadets, 12, 96, 97
  Cycling Team, 130–31
  Dining Services, 74
  Drone Park, 24, 161
  Foundation, 19, 86, 147
  Innovation Campus, 23, 151, 170–71
  Mid-Atlantic Aviation Partnership (MAAP), 23, 160–61
  Montgomery Executive Airport, 17, 18, 85
  name, 1, 2, 9, 10, 17
  Northern Virginia Center, 19, 171
  presidents and Confederate ties, 4, 8, 30,
  Principles of Community, 21–22, 91, 103
  school colors, 9, 118

Science Festival, 149
seal, 3, 9
Transportation Institute, 19, 151, 162–63
Women's Center, 104

Walker, Gilbert C., 2, 4, 6
Wake Forest University, 20, 119
Wallace, Maude, 45
War Memorial Chapel, Court, and Pylons, ii, 13, 14, 82, 98–99, 113, 121
War Memorial Gymnasium and Hall, 12, 63, 86
Warner, Mark, 88–89
West, Hattie P., 67
White, Robin, 138
Whitehurst, James Leslie, Jr., 25
Whitehurst Hall, 25
William and Mary, 122
Williams Hall, 17, 98
Wills, George, 119

Women; admission to Virginia Tech, ix, 10, 12–13, 14, 15, 17, 58, 59, 61, 83; athletics, 19–20, 126–27, 128–29; campus housing, 13; enslaved African people at Smithfield and Solitude, 2, 29; faculty and staff at Virginia Tech, 13, 136–37, 138, 154–55, 174; first graduates, 12, 60; and homecoming, 116–17, 178; and Radford College, 14, 16–17; and Virginia Cooperative Extension, 10, 45, 46–47; and Virginia Tech Corps of Cadets, 12, 96, 97; and the Women's Center, 104; and the Women's Student Organization, 12
World War I, 12, 33, 57, 63
World War II, 13–14, 77, 78
WUVT, 86
WVTF, 86

Yates, Charlie L., 15, 80–81
YMCA Building, 85